DISTANCE LEARNING

ARTICLES

1 APPROACHES TOWARD DIGITAL STRATIFIED PROJECT-BASED LEARNING
Leonard Hammer

11 STUDENT SUPPORT SERVICE IN VIRTUAL LEARNING ENVIRONMENTS: McKENNA CONTENT ANALYSIS METHOD
Mojgan Mohammadimehr, Mohsen Keshavarz, and Zohrehsadat Mirmoghtadaie*

25 STUDENTS, PRESENTATIONS, AND THE PANDEMIC: RESTRUCTURING ASSIGNMENTS, AND ASSESSMENT
Cheyenne Seymour

33 SMILE, WINK, LAUGH: INCORPORATING EMOJIS TO INCREASE STUDENTS' PERCEPTION OF INSTRUCTOR HUMANNESS IN AN ONLINE SPANISH COURSE
Shelly Wyatt and María T. Redmon

45 EVALUATION AND INVESTIGATION OF PRESCIENCE TEACHERS' PERCEPTIONS TOWARD DISTANCE EDUCATION
Nesrin Ürün Arici and Emre Yildiz

COLUMNS

ENDS AND MEANS
Preparing for and Cultivating Instructional Continuity in Online Courses   55
—by Natalie B. Milman

TRY THIS
Labor-Based Grading: Perfect for Distance Learning!   59
—by Errol Craig Sull

ASK ERROL!   63
—by Errol Craig Sull

AND FINALLY ...
Interactive Instructional Videos   68
—by Michael Simonson

Volume 19, Issue 1   **Distance Learning**   i

EDITOR
Michael Simonson
simsmich@nova.edu

EMERITUS EDITOR
Charles Schlosser

MANAGING EDITOR
Kathleen Hagen
khagen@nova.edu

ASSISTANT EDITOR FOR SOCIAL MEDIA
Deborah Seepersaud
dseepersaud@barry.edu

ASSOCIATION EDITOR
Reggie Smith
rsmith@usdla.org

PUBLISHER
Information Age Publishing
216 W. North Main Street
2nd Floor
Waxhaw, NC 28173
(704) 752-9125
www.infoagepub.com

ADVERTISING
United States Distance Learning Association
10 G Street, NE Suite 600
Washington, DC 20002
202-248-5023

EDITORIAL OFFICES
Fischler College of Education and School of Criminal Justice
Nova Southeastern University
3301 College Ave.
Fort Lauderdale, FL 33314
954-262-8563
FAX 954-262-3724
simsmich@nova.edu

PURPOSE
Distance Learning, an official publication of the United States Distance Learning Association (USDLA), is sponsored by the USDLA, by the Fischler College of Education at Nova South-eastern University, and by Information Age Publishing. Distance Learning is published four times a year for leaders, practitioners, and decision makers in the fields of distance learning, e-learning, telecommunications, and related areas. It is a professional magazine with information for those who provide instruction to all types of learners, of all ages, using telecommunications technologies of all types. Articles are written by practitioners for practitioners with the intent of providing usable information and ideas for readers. Articles are accepted from authors with interesting and important information about the effective practice of distance teaching and learning.

SPONSORS
The United States Distance Learning (USDLA) is the professional organization for those involved in distance teaching and learning. USDLA is committed to being the leading distance learning association in the United States. USDLA serves the needs of the distance learning community by providing advocacy, information, networking and opportunity. www.usdla.org

INFORMATION AGE PUBLISHING
216 W. North Main Street,
2nd Floor
Waxhaw, NC 28173
(704) 752-9125
www.infoagepub.com

SUBSCRIPTIONS
Members of the United States Distance Learning Association receive *Distance Learning* as part of their membership. Others may subscribe to *Distance Learning*.
Individual Subscription: $60
Institutional Subscription: $175
Student Subscription: $40

DISTANCE LEARNING RESOURCE INFORMATION:
Visit http://www.usdla.org/html/resources/dlmag/index.htm
Advertising Rates and Information:
617-399-1770, x11
Subscription Information:
Contact USDLA at
617-399-1770
info@usdla.org

DISTANCE LEARNING
is indexed by the Blended, Online Learning and Distance Education (BOLDE) research bank.

DISTANCE LEARNING JOURNAL
PUBLISHING GUIDELINES
EMAIL SUBMISSIONS

MANUSCRIPT PREPARATION GUIDELINES

Articles are accepted from authors with interesting and important information about the effective practice of distance teaching and learning. No page costs are charged authors, nor are stipends paid. Two copies of the issue with the author's article will be provided. Reprints will also be available.

1. Manuscript's should be written in Microsoft Word, saved as a .doc file or docx file, and sent using email.

2. *Single* space the entire manuscript. Use 12-point Times New Roman (TNR) font.

3. Margins: 1" on all sides.

4. Do not use any subheadings, page numbers, or embedded commands. Documents that have embedded commands will be returned.

5. Include a cover sheet with the paper's title and with the names, affiliations and addresses of all authors. High resolution professional photographs of all authors should be included and should have a **file size larger than 500kb**.

6. Submit the paper via email attachment that is clearly marked. The name of the manuscript file should reference the author. Submissions should be sent marked ATTENTION *Distance Learning* submission.

7. Send email submissions to:
   simsmich@nova.edu
   Michael R. Simonson
   Editor

Distance Learning journal
Fischler College of Education and
School of Criminal Justice
Nova Southeastern University
4118 DeSantis Building
3301 College Avenue
Fort Lauderdale, FL 33314

The Manuscript

Word Processor Format
Manuscripts should be written in Microsoft Word.

Length
There is no page length. The average manuscript is between 3,000 and 5,000 words.

Text
Regular text: 12 point TNR, left justified.

Do not type section headings or titles in all-caps, only capitalize the first letter in each word of a title. Allow one line of space before and after each heading. Indent, 0.5", the first sentence of each paragraph.

Figures and Tables
Figures and tables should fit width 6½" and be incorporated into the document.

Page Numbering
Do not include or refer to any page numbers in your manuscript.

Graphics
We encourage you to use visuals—pictures, graphics, figures, charts—to help explain your article. Graphics images (.jpg) should be included at the end of your paper. Graphic images should be at least 500 kb in size.

Get Your Copy Today—Information Age Publishing

IN UPCOMING ISSUES

Application and Feasibility of Various Teaching Tools Used in Online Classes During COVID-19 in Tertiary Education	Sumie Chan
Demystifying the User Experience of K–5 Students With a Digital Book Application	Dalal Alfageh Fatih Demir
The Relationship of Scaffolding, Time, Page Views and Grades	John Griffith Emily Faulconer
Is it Convenience? Investigating Factors That Influence Graduate Students' Preference for Method of Online Lecture Participation	Adam Ladwig Patti J. Berg-Poppe Moses Ikiugu Brandon M. Ness
Moving to Emergency Remote Teaching	Parama Chaudhuri

Approaches Toward Digital Stratified Project-Based Learning

Leonard Hammer

This article reviews different approaches toward a stratified form of project-based learning (PBL) in a digital environment. Recognizing that a variety of participatory layers enriches the classroom PBL experience, the article reviews different formats of stratified PBL that were utilized in a variety of courses. The central point of this review is to point out the importance of accounting for the desired course focus and outcomes and the benefits of providing a stratified form of PBL for students as grounds for further enriching project engagement and content.

INTRODUCTION

Project-based learning (PBL) is a content-based activity composed of a series of tasks to solve problems,

Leonard Hammer,
Director of Outreach and Development,
Human Rights Practice Program,
University of Arizona.
Phone: 1 (520) 834-5503
Email: lhammer@email.arizona.edu

think critically, make decisions, produce products, and articulate the process and products (Beckett & Slater, 2020). As such, PBL has become a key mechanism to enrich student learning and broaden forms of engagement. PBL provides broader vistas for students to acquire knowledge and insight into their areas of focus, socializes learners through real-world activities that afford opportunities to learn subject matter, social cultures, critical thinking, decision making, and collaborative work skills, and affords a broader and richer platform from which to learn about applications of the materials under examination, as well as begin to achieve practical solutions to the issues they are analyzing in the classroom (Barnes, 2015; Ward-Penny, 2010). PBL also affords opportunities for cross-departmental and interdisciplinary studies through a variety of project work that might entail social justice projects using specific language skills or STEM-oriented projects that require an understanding of the geography, societies, or cultures examined.

Of course, to make PBL a successful enterprise, students must be provided with adequate direction, the proper construct of projects, clear focus, and a working infrastructure that allows for the flow of information between students, among involved faculty, and of course with the project providers themselves (when using external source providers for projects). As noted by Elliot and Bikowski (2020), PBL is a particularly strong tool that is enhanced when class framework and materials are designed with a clear strategy that supports the goal(s) of the class and the use of PBL.

The beneficial factors of PBL can be even further enhanced when engaged within the digital realm given the capacity for an even broader scope of engagement and deeper and richer understanding of materials beyond the physical confines of a region or area where a student might reside, thus opening up more possibilities for project work, and understanding issues and problems learned in the classroom in an even deeper and richer context (Bax, 2011; Macgilchrist et al., 2020; Thomas, 2017). Thus digital PBL allows injecting more varied and richer layers and strata into the educational mix, be it through the projects taken on by students, involvement of foreign students from different regions and with differing world views, or involvement of other faculty and departments where digital platforms allow for broader and more varied forms of instruction and engagement. As noted by Pegrum (2009):

> Digital technologies lend themselves to constructivist, collaborative pedagogies ... while we can't imagine much less guarantee what the jobs of the future will be, we can be fairly sure that they will occur in postindustrial contexts, will involve digital technologies, and will require multiple literacies. And notwithstanding the crucial need for balance, we can be fairly sure that social constructivism and related pedagogies provide good preparation for these conditions, helping students develop relevant skill sets—and open mindsets. (p. 54)

The author added that it is not just a matter of preparation for securing employment.

> However, it is also imperative to acquire adequate digital literacy whereby education must also prepare students for a social future where they have the technological and personal literacies to build their own digital identities and author their narratives. It must prepare them for a sociopolitical future where they have the participatory and remix literacies to intervene in social narratives. (p. 54)

What emerges is that the digital realm of PBL can meet the goals of preparing students for a digital presence by creating a stratified form of project learning given the variety of layers that are available and involved for the institution(s), the student(s), and the project providers in entering and utilizing the digital realm. It is especially important when factoring in the globalized world in which we operate and the strong intermix of disciplines, ideas, and approaches that regularly occurs within the marketplace, be it in the sciences, businesses, or otherwise. The digital environment for PBL affords a richer fabric of potential project work for students. One can work across institutions from different regions, thus opening up possibilities beyond merely cross-disciplinary work and different perspectives and approaches within the same discipline.

Stratified PBL in the digital environment also integrates students from wildly different backgrounds and perspectives that allow them to think and work together on a project in a manner that would not occur should they merely share the same classroom or Zoom room, with little or no actual interaction. Further, stratified PBL opens up vistas for project providers from different regions to integrate into digital PBL across institutions. This opportunity provides an even deeper layer of perspective and more opportunities for socially disadvantaged or disconnected communities who might have previously lacked access or even a voice in engaging needed project work, access to labs or technology, or the capacity and infrastructure to move a project forward. Stratified PBL affords faculty and students an exciting opportunity to engage differing social and cultural approaches, incorporates diverse political boundaries and perspectives, and seamlessly interweaves the economic layers of the global South and North to emerge with students and faculty working with a diverse stratum of people and projects that further enriches the PBL process.

A wide variety of avenues and experiential options have become available for PBL, especially for project providers and their needs and desires to engage students in projects. In addition, the wide availability of MOOCs and online webinars and workshops can further enrich the classroom and open up even more vistas and possibilities for student projects (Ellis, 2009). These digital possibilities become even more enmeshed with broader reaches outside a particular region or continent. Furthermore, as digital technology is further applied to the PBL framework allowing for more engagement (Thomas & Yamazaki, 2021), it is worth considering the different methods and approaches utilized by stratified PBL to account for the different operative frameworks and constructs that meet the needs classrooms and institutions. The underlying goal, of course, is to interject diverse layers and strata of views and directions to a project that benefits one's students, such as achieving the desired outcomes and learning objectives of a particular course and adequately preparing them for an intermixed and intermeshed world. It is worth noting some approaches that allow for a preconceived approach to stratified PBL that best conforms to the goals of the lecturer and course.

PREDEFINED NEEDS

The various approaches noted in this article derive from courses created by the author at the University of Arizona's Human Rights Practice graduate program (HRt). The HRt is a wholly online human rights program that already had the framework for externalizing PBL in the digital format. The program further relied on external guest lectures to enrich course materials, open up avenues for project work, and allow the students to experience the ways and means of actual human rights practice. PBL is a seminal component of the program as it is geared to encourage student experiences in the real world and involve students in ongoing group project work, be it on actual projects or in analyzing human rights practices of organizations. The use of projects by outside providers and guest lecturers worldwide reflects the ethos of the HRt program to incorporate voices and views from around the world and offer support where feasible to nongovernmental organizations (NGOs) and community groups through guest lecturing fees and assistive PBL project work. The PBL component and group work of usually three to four students entails students working with the instructor and community members on real-world issues from around the globe.

Given the preexisting structure in the HRt program, we adopt different approaches for greater student networking with students from outside the program and with human rights practitioners to interject more diverse and critical methods toward projects that reflect and incorporate real-world applications of the materials the students are learning. Thus emerged a more stratified form of PBL whereby the goal is to incorporate a host of different approaches toward a particular problem, allowing for different strata of views to be incorporated into completing projects. The different strata of approaches emerge from the project providers, the institutions involved, and the different students involved in the project itself. Furthermore, this collaboration is all actualized through the digital space. The result is that a stratified approach to PBL affords students a broad and rich view of how social contexts and cultural backgrounds implement project work. PBL leads to a more critical approach to project work that incorporates viewpoints and diverse perceptions that impact project fulfillment. It is worth considering the different frameworks created for stratified PBL approach that demonstrates the pluses and minuses of using a stratified form of PBL in a digital environment.

INTEGRATING PBL INTO THE STRUCTURE

An example of a less layered form of PBL in a digital environment is the strategic litigation seminar that initiated the notion of stratified PBL. It involved NGOs and assistive project work according to their needs and wants in providing the HRt program with PBL projects. It is important to note that projects emanate from outside providers, thus creating richer layers as the instructor and students are provided real-world projects with meaning and actual need. (In the case of the HRt, it usually derives from various NGOs and civil society organizations from around the world). Note, too, that the strategic litigation course's focus was to demonstrate to nonlaw students studying international human rights law that there are many ways to engage and utilize human rights law as a tool beyond just the courtroom or before governmental operatives. As such, the course created connections between the students and different NGOs to work on projects involving the application of human rights norms in different ways, including ways in which to engage the public and notify them of their rights, or mobilize a group of people in understanding and thinking of ways to actually rely upon and socially implement human rights law for their benefit. For example, an NGO providing legal aid services for vulnerable populations in Bishkek, Kyrgyzstan, was having difficulty meeting the needs of the number of domestic violence victims seeking their services. The project taken on by the students explored best practices for providing holistic legal aid along with psychological and other forms of domestic social services, with the result being a white paper that served as a guiding instrument for the NGO to expand their services and involve other professions in a pro-bono manner. The idea here was to allow students to see a broader form of application of human rights law in a manner where they were involved in a specific project, all within a digital environment. This project afforded them an understanding and insight into their capacities to create change and involve organizations and others in a meaningful manner.

Granted, this was a low-pressure project as the students were requested to utilize their ideas and approaches for a variety of NGOs issues of how to tackle problems they faced and how best to make use of the digital environment for their benefit (for instance, domestic violence among an indigenous population in a remote rural area, creating hotlines with direct connections to the police). Nevertheless, it was a good way to integrate outside project providers, show them what can be done, and open up opportunities for students to intern. Thus the layers were not necessarily that deep in this case. However, it did entail students engaging the outside world and added a nice layer of external involvement that enhanced the PBL experience by involving NGOs and project providers from overseas, where their issues or projects involved matters that might seem routine or obvious to U.S. students.

The most challenging aspect of this PBL experience, an issue that prevails for all forms of PBL in a digital environment, is tracking the projects and maintaining oversight of the students and their work as they progress forward. Maintaining oversight is especially difficult in a digital environment, where creating the connection between the project provider and the student is essential to ensure communication and proper project implementation. As the instructor, one must ensure seamless communication and project completion. Thus, ongoing meetings and sessions between students and the instructor, and the instructor and project provider, are just as important as those between the students and the project provider. The instructor is advised to meet with the students regularly, sit in on student group meetings as a quiet bystander, meet with the project provider for assessment at least three times during the duration of the course, sit in as a quiet observer when students meet with the project provider, and constantly ensure oversight of project work as it emerges. It is also advisable to have the different student groups meet, describe their work, and be open for comments and input from other students (thus further enriching the available strata being offered). An end-of-semester presentation by the students to each other is offered so they might see their work come to fruition.

The strategic litigation course served as a model to demonstrate to the students and lecturers involved in the HRt program that this was attainable and possible in a digital environment. Students and lecturers began to incorporate the idea, especially as the program made extensive and ongoing use of integrating guest lecturers into the lecturing portions, requesting the guest lecturers for projects that the students might participate in and assist in engaging human rights practice. Thus, the project work carried out under the strategic litigation course paved the way for genuinely varied stratified PBL through integrated lessons with different universities from around the globe and student group involvement from different universities and regions intermixing and interlinking with each other through the PBL projects, as explained below.

THEME-ORIENTED STRATIFIED PBL

The next form of stratified PBL provided deeper layers but within a specific theme of project work. Although the theme was uniform, the projects and regions in which the PBL manifested were quite varied and involved a variety of places and countries, all with their specific issues surrounding the chosen theme. In this case, the HRt program took on the matter of housing rights as a common thematic issue to be addressed in the PBL context. A common theme makes it easier to involve students from different universities and regions as they have a prechosen subject and focus and thus (usually) have a keen interest in the subject and desire to tackle the issue through project work. Further, the projects could delve deeper into the issue leading to more meaningful applications (thus enriching the layers of the stratified PBL). The instructor was able to teach the students specific content focus for projects surrounding housing rights, enabling them to be prepared and project ready. Oversight of the PBL projects was also easier as the students more readily understood the issues and materials and could jump right into the projects. In this instance, the project providers were NGOs doing work in the housing rights sector around the world (including India, Central Asia, and the United States), and they proved to be solid guest lecturers as well for lecture content. We added in additional strata to the groups by having students from the American University of Central Asia (AUCA) in Bishkek, Kyrgyzstan, join the lectures and group work, thus serving as a litmus test to the scope of stratified PBL that can be undertaken before deepening and involving more layers of participants. Interestingly, the AUCA students were from different disciplines (law and international relations), thus affording even richer layers of insights and expertise to the group projects being undertaken.

The common theme of the projects made this endeavor more manageable. Notably, the common theme form of stratified PBL allowed for preconceived projects with clear outcomes to achieve, as per the needs of the project providers. The benefit of a theme-oriented PBL focused course then is that oversight of the student and their projects prove easier as one can have the students engage each other. Different groups comment on their work and the work of other groups in a more substantive fashion and offer insights, along with the lecturer of the course, thus placing the students on equal footing with the instructor (and sometimes even surpassing the instructor as the students delved further into the issues and projects at hand). Further, it made for a tighter and unifying fit within the course. Students became more proficient in the materials and understood the problems at hand and the projects being undertaken. Thus, the common-theme stratified PBL was quite satisfying for the student groups despite being from different institutions and disciplines. Using a common theme also pleased the project providers because the students felt confident and able to tackle the issues, all while contributing their ideas, approaches, and perceptions of the issue that further enriched the project content and afforded even more varied layers to the ideas being developed. Students emerged with projects centering on the ways and means to uphold housing rights that differed for each region and country under examination. In some instances, students provided toolkits on how to protect themselves from forced eviction and, in other instances mobilizing groups of people in areas targeted by governments for expropriation to begin to involve and engage local politicians. They reflected the importance of allowing for regional and cultural considerations when thinking about enforcing or moving for the application of the housing rights.

MULTINODAL STRATIFIED PBL

The next step for further developing an enriched stratified PBL was to engage a multinodal approach to instruction and course content. We integrated students from different disciplines and departments, three different institutions, and a wide variety of project topics, albeit within the social justice context). The multinodal extensively used the digital platform for stratified PBL by involving three different universities and five departments (that intermixed undergraduate and graduate students). This project was first accomplished by reaching out to a different department entirely at the University of Arizona, the Russian and Slavic Studies (RSS) Department. RSS had been engaged in the form of stratified PBL in the digital environment through their Russian language course, relying on the digital environment to have their students engage Russian-speaking project providers to practice their language skills. RSS desired to integrate social justice projects for students to work on. It was but a natural fit to ameliorate the RSS undergraduate students with the HRt graduate students to work on projects that would play to the strengths of each program, as we decided to engage project providers in the Central Asian region.

There were key distinct advantages offered by the relationship between RSS and HRt, aside from an opportunity to enrich the involved student layers within the stratified PBL given the different disciplines being folded into the student groups. Advantages included leveraged contacts from each department that would allow for a wider variety of projects to be offered, the different insights and approaches that each department maintained that allowed for richer content and more structured output for the students, and the fact that each department desired cross-cultural engagement as each recognized the benefits provided by such exchanges for learning capacitation for the students and PBL. Further, given the work of the HRt program in Russia and Central Asia and the capacity of RSSS students to use the lingua franca of the area and intermesh socially and culturally, the desire to work together was quite stark. The inherent ethos of each program was to have students involved in stratified PBL, with a strong desire to create rich layers of social and cultural perspectives, thereby allowing for exposure to a variety of viewpoints and approaches toward a particular problem.

Given that HRts had already created a relationship with AUCA through the common-theme stratified PBL (as well as, on a smaller scale, we had been conducting a summer strategic litigation course on human rights with AUCA students and other students from the Central Asian region that created even stronger ties), both HRt and AUCA students were already used to having lectures from both faculty in a digital format, as well as having guest lectures from external NGOs. However, another layer was added by RSS: students and faculty in International Relations from the University of Saint Peter the Great in Saint Petersburg, Russia, whose students were particularly keen to work with fellow students from around the world on social justice issues.

Given the wide net of contacts for all programs and institutions involved in this multimodal approach to stratified PBL, we connected with NGOs in Kyrgyzstan, Uzbekistan, Turkmenistan, and Kazakhstan who provided a variety of different project work for the students. Projects ranged from environmental matters focusing on ecotourism, domestic violence and providing social protections, socially mobilizing different population groups, and assisting in the work of a parliamentary watchdog that provided oversight for ensuring democratic practices by the national government.

Although this was not entirely predecided, it turned out that the projects all would focus on creating different forms of podcasts for various use by the project providers (some as citizen information, some for their own NGOs, and others for politicians and activists in the area). As such, we engaged another node to further enrich the PBL by having guest lectures from a leading NGO that worked on narrative creation and the means of engaging audiences. Given in English, this provided another outlet for utilizing the Russian language skills of the RSS and the English skills of the students from Russia and Kyrgyzstan. We further added even another strata by having guest lectures from UA professors from the Fine Arts Department who worked on media and documentary films and from Journalism who specialized in podcast creation. These strata were further enriched by having two graduates of the HRt program talk to the students about their capstone projects that had involved the use of podcasting as a form of social mobilization and engagement.

Thus, various lectures integrated the nodes between external NGOs who were relevant guest lecturers and the faculty nodes of different departments and institutions. This assimilation allowed for richer discussions between students and faculty in common online lecture rooms. It allowed the students to get to know one another as a precursor to forming groups and working on projects. The project providers then engaged the students from three different regions, with the students knowing the desired end product (creating a podcast on a particular issue and with a particular goal in mind). As above, oversight and ongoing engagement were key. However, this time, the meetings between groups were incredible as the students were teaching others (and the instructors) about the issues. Different groups offered fresh eyes and insights into the projects, thus further enriching the strata being engaged for the project. Intergroup meetings were held three times during the semester, and the eventual podcasts were made available to all students.

What is unique about the multinodal approach to stratified PBL is that depending on the form by which the lecturing takes place, additional nodes can be added at will, thereby further enhancing and deepening the available strata. These nodes can be focused on project providers, institutions, departments, fields, or regions, all according to the instructor's needs and desired direction(s) and the manner and form of depth that is to be added to the stratified PBL framework. Given the advent of guest lecturers, who can further enhance the lectures and afford additional insights into the materials and the projects that are to take place, the capacity to add on even more nodes is quite illuminating. The different nodes (be it of students, institutions, project providers, regions, or lecturers) are all connected by virtue of shared activities (principally lecturing and PBL project work) as well as shared project work (between intuitions and project providers) that further enriches the stratified PBL taking place. The nodal system allows participating institutions and departments to track activities, allow for further faculty exchange of ideas and lecturing, maintain departmental autonomy (as some departments might desire to stress specific activities, such as language development, while others in media might desire to focus on podcast creation or create a wholly different focus depending on the departments or institutions involved as well as the discipline and activity undertaken), and affords a broader picture for student involvement as they too understand the relationships being developed.

Conclusion

Stratified PBL can be implemented in a variety of formats. The central point is that the result was all the same in each; students felt enriched by what they were learning and enjoyed the formats being offered. As we delved into the multinodal format, we were unsure if it would enhance learning outcomes and if students would even enjoy engaging students and project providers from such a broad array of areas, approaches, and disciplines. Much to our surprise, the students across the board clamored for these forms of interactions as they recognized that this was the approach they would be taking in their future careers. Students felt emboldened with ideas and new vistas, given their interactions with such a diverse group of people. They appreciated the building up of additional strata to the PBL projects, and it more accurately mirrored their world and encapsulated a world in which they desired to engage.

Of course, the format depends on the scope and capacity of individual departments and institutions. However, the beauty of a digital format for stratified PBL is that the possibilities are endless and can be accomplished seamlessly given proper preparation, clear focus, and maintenance of the desired learning outcomes. All of these are central elements to any format of stratified PBL as they filter down both to the students engaging the projects and the projects providers as well, thus leading to successful results and satisfied participants from all sides.

References

Barnes, J. (2015). *Cross-curricular learning*. SAGE.

Bax, S. (2011). Digital education: Beyond the "wow" factor. In M. Thomas (Ed.), *Digital education: Opportunities for social collaboration* (pp. 239–256). Palgrave.

Beckett, G., & Slater, T. (Eds). (2020). *Global perspectives on project-based language learning, teaching, and assessment: Key approaches, technology tools, and frameworks*. Routledge.

Ellis, R. (2009). Task-based language teaching: Sorting out the misunderstandings. *International Journal of Applied Linguistics, 19(3)*, 221–246.

Elliot, J., & Bikowski, D. (2020). Framework for learning with digital resources applications for project-based language learning. In G. Beckett & T. Slater (Eds.), *Global perspectives on project-based language learning, teaching, and assessment: Key approaches, technology tools, and frameworks* (pp. 167–185). Routledge.

Macgilchrist, F., Allert, H., & Bruch, A. (2020). Students and society in the 2020s: Three future "histories" of education and technology. *Learning, Media and Technology, 45*(1), 76–89.

Pegrum, M. (2009). *From blogs to bombs: The future of digital technologies in education.* (ebook). University of Western Australia.

Thomas, M. (2017). *Project-based language learning with technology: Learner collaboration in an EFL classroom in Japan.* Routledge.

Thomas, M., & Yamazaki, K. (Eds.). (2021). Introduction: Projects, pandemics and the re-positioning of digital language learning. In *Project-based language learning and CALL: From virtual exchange to social justice* (pp. 1–18). University of Toledo.

Ward-Penny, R. (2010). *Cross-curricular teaching and learning in the secondary school ... mathematics.* Routledge.

Student Support Service in Virtual Learning Environments

McKenna Content Analysis Method

Mojgan Mohammadimehr, Mohsen Keshavarz, Zohrehsadat Mirmoghtadaie[*]

Student support services are a broad and important concept in education. This study aims to explain the student support system in virtual learning environments. This study was a qualitative research project. An extensive search in scientific databases was carried out based on predetermined strategies, and 53 documents were reviewed from 1996 until 2019. Data were analyzed based on Hugh McKenna's 9-step approach. According to the literature review, determining students' support services in virtual learning and providing academic and nonacademic services is the responsibility of students' cognitive, emotional, and social needs. These services lead to greater student participation in self-learning and academic achievement, which is done at 3 levels: (preprogram, learning

Mojgan Mohammadimehr,
Associate Professor, Department of Laboratory Sciences, Faculty of Paramedical Sciences, AJA University of Medical Sciences, Tehran, Iran.
Email: M.mohammadimehr@ajaums.ac.ir

Mohsen Keshavarz,
Assistance Professor, Department of E-Learning in Medical Sciences, School of Paramedical Sciences, Torbat Heydariyeh University of Medical Sciences, Torbat Heydariyeh, Iran.
Email: keshavarzm1@thums.ac.ir

process, and postgraduate support services). Student support services in virtual learning can be divided into academic and nonacademic. Policymakers can use these results for different types of virtual learning.

Keywords: student support service, virtual learning, content analysis, environment

INTRODUCTION

The internet provides the basis for new learning environments called "virtual learning" (Shieh & Yu, 2016). The world is becoming more interconnected and complex, and online learning is going through a period of rapid and unprecedented change. The following e-learning trends and predictions for 2020 will help us prepare for this space (Lopez-Catalan & Bañuls, 2017). Medical education is a process that continues throughout the life of medical students, and the development of information has made medical science knowledge constantly evolving. As a result, the knowledge and skills gained at the end of academic education cannot guarantee the skills needed during the individual's lifetime. Therefore, medical students need to acquire more skills during education, such as self-directed learning to lifelong learning (Duffy & Holmboe, 2006).

Due to the benefits of virtual education and its effective impact on medical education, it seems mandatory to incorporate it into the current curriculum so that conventional teaching methods are a combination of traditional education and e-learning (Frehywot et al., 2013; Liu et al., 2014). Blended learning is an educational approach that combines online educational materials and opportunities for interaction online with traditional place-based classroom methods. Using a combination of digital instruction and one-on-one Face-Time, students can work on their own with new concepts that free up teachers to circulate and support individual students who may need individualized attention.

> Rather than playing to the lowest common denominator—as they would in a traditional classroom—teachers can now streamline their instruction to help all students reach their full potential. Working in a blended learning environment requires high flexibility. (Wikipedia, 2019)

The width and depth of distance learning depend on the objectives and prospects of this type of education based on upstream policies (Lenar et al., 2014). For many reasons, such as the complexity of this learning environment, all the learners cannot perform this responsibility as fully as possible. Some do not achieve success and satisfaction due to the lack of requirements management (Yukselturk & Yildirim, 2008). Student support is a generic term used for a wide range of services. It

Zohrehsadat Mirmoghtadaiẽ,
Assistance Professor, Department of e-Learning, Virtual School of Medical Education and Management, Shahid Beheshti University of Medical Sciences, Tehran, Iran.
Email: mirmoghtada@sbmu.ac.ir

offers by institutions to help students acquire and develop learning objectives and achieve knowledge, attitudes, and skills (Arko-Achemfuor, 2017).

Support services are a crucial element for all educational institutions; however, these services are much more essential in e-learning than face to face. One of the most important reasons is that teachers and students are not in a physical environment, and distance learning sessions usually require more interpersonal interactions than group interactions (Kumtepe et al., 2003). Some learners feel lonely. In addition, some students stop attending class or drop out of college due to the lack of self-management skills, motivation, and a sense of belonging to their institution. Student support services have emerged as an important element of the distance education system (Chatpakkarattana & Khlaisang, 2013). Although emphasizing active learners support systems, the new courses facilitate the learning process through learning tools and services (Cheawjindakarn et al., 2013; Usun, 2004). The development of an organization-based support system is accomplished through several techniques. The main focus of this support system is on the satisfaction and facilitation of learners (Cheawjindakarn, 2013). Much research shows that comprehensive support for education can lead to academic well-being. Academic well-being is the attitude of students to education. This attitude has meaning in four dimensions: the general attitude to the academic life, the attitude to the teacher, the attitude to the peers, and the attitude to the organizational structure of colleges (Unwin, 2009). In many studies, the impact of support service on students' well-being has been demonstrated, but what are the dimensions and components of the concept of support in blended learning? There is very little research in this field, and it only has focused on when the student support service should be activated (Tamulienė, 2014). There is no specific support mechanism in blended learning. In this study, concept analysis has been used to identify student service dimensions and refine basic conceptual components to provide a clear and practical definition.

METHOD

SEARCH STRATEGY CONCEPT ANALYSIS

The search strategy of this concept analysis included a protocol-driven search. Original articles, as well as theoretical and conceptual articles, were consulted. We looked at peer-reviewed papers in all fields. Nine databases were searched (ProQuest, ERIC, Google Scholar, Science Direct, Scopus, Medline, ISI, ISC, and web of science) with the following keywords entered: support system, support service, education support system, training support, practical or emotional support system, and academic support, learner support, student support service, smart support service, e-support, faculty support system. The search terms above were combined with the following terms: distance learning, e-learning, blended learning, virtual learning, distance education, computer enhanced learning, online education, and online class.

ELIGIBILITY CRITERIA

In the literature review, 1,872 related articles available on the databases from 1996 until 2019 were found. Therefore, a data management strategy was developed; the search was limited to articles that listed the search terms in their title. At first, abstracts of the study articles were selected, and articles that described the concept or provided evidence related to the concept were selected for the full-text study. No further assessment of the validity or quality of the full text was conducted. Two peers screened all the definitions from the same research unit and evaluated the definitions' appropriateness. Finally, 53 documents were reviewed (Figure 1).

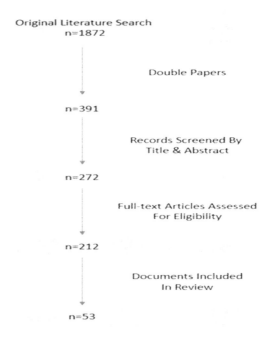

Figure 1. The search process and inclusion of papers in this review.

CONCEPT ANALYSIS

Conceptual analysis is a precise process that attempts to identify, clarify, and explain an abstract concept and distinguish it from similar concepts (McKenna, 2006; Morse et al., 1991; Schwartz-Barcott & Kim, 2000; Walker & Avant, 2005). There are different approaches in this study; the Hugh McKenna approach is used for concept analysis. The analysis was comprised of the nine steps shown in Figure 2.

RESULTS

DEFINITIONS

Support service is a complex concept; it can be approached from several perspectives (the students, teachers, or the education system) that lead to different dimensions. There was a nonobvious distinction between academic support, learner support, faculty support system, education support system, e-support, training support, smart support service, support service, or emotional support system in context from reliable sources. At this stage, reference phrases, also known as primary concept structures, were extracted from the existing documentation, that is, the exact sentences were quoted. In the next stage, we introduced our interpretation of primary phrases. Then we introduced our interpretation of primary phrases in documentation as the potential attributes that define the concept of support service. Some attributes of the concept are repeated frequently. This stage was performed with high accuracy, and the specific attributes of the concept were extracted.

1	• Selecting a suitable concept for concept analysis onset • In this step, we answer the question "what are the elements and structures of student support concept?"
2	• Determining and defining the purpose of concept analysis • At this step, the aim is to explain the elements and structures of the student support concept.
3	• Identifying and specifying the meaning of the concept • In this step, the fields that include student support concept were identified
4	• Determining the attributes that define the concept • After reviewing the fields related to the student support concept, new classification establish.
5	• Identifying and implementing a model case • A model is a pure example that the student support concept is used in it and should have all the features of the concept.
6	• Identifying and implementing a variety of cases such as contrary, borderline, related, invented, illegitimate and false cases • Alternative cases include examples of what is not the student support concept.
7	• Identification of antecedents and consequences of the concept • In this step, the analysis of the field is used.
8	• Noticing contexts and values • concepts have different meanings based on the context. Therefore the role of student support in every country relates to context and values.
9	• Identification and designation of the empirical indicators of the concept • This step is considered as the operationalization of student support concept

Figure 2. Hugh McKenna's nine-step method for concept analysis.

Therefore, the purpose of student supportive service in blended learning is to provide academic and nonacademic services that respond to students' cognitive, affective, and social needs. These services lead to further engaging the student in self-learning and academic achievement. They are performed at three levels: preprogram, learning process, and postgraduation support services. Based on resources that discussed support service, the main components of this concept were determined as follows: supportive service levels, supportive service Dimensions, and supportive service purposes (Figure 3).

LEVELS OF STUDENT SUPPORTIVE SERVICE

The study of the texts showed that this field has three separate parts: preprogram support services, the learning process support services, and postgraduation, shown in Table 1.

PREPROGRAM STUDENT SUPPORT SERVICES

Moreover, institutions in the education sector are expected to use information and communication technologies effectively to succeed in educational activities and programs. At this phase, entry requirements and all rules and regulations of the academic calendar will be announced. These items illustrate the college's commitment to programs and facilitate decision-making for students.

LEARNING PROCESS STUDENT SUPPORT SERVICES

The development of a learning support service for distance learning during the academic years includes: (1) establishing and improving information media, (2) exploring learning strategies for learners, and (3) access to all digital resources. If support services are further developed, learning outcomes will clearly improve (Lehtinen et al., 1999). The support

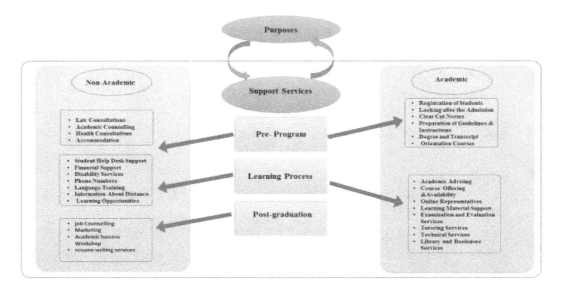

Figure 3. Student supportive service in blended learning: Levels, dimensions, and purposes.

Table 1. Levels of Student Supportive Service and References

Levels of Student Supportive Service	References
Preprogram support services	• Kumtepe et al. (2003) • Floyd & Casey-Powell (2004) • Gujjar et al. (2010) • Chatpakkarattana & Khlaisang (2012) • Jain et al. (2016) • Sahoo (2018)
The learning process support services	• Tait (2000) • Kumtepe (2003) • LaPadula (2003) • Darojat & Sunarsih (2014) • Nurmukhametov et al. (2015) • Arko-Achemfuor (2017) • Lu & Luo (2017) • Sánchez-Elvira Paniagua & Simpson (2018)
Postgraduation support services	• Floyd & Casey-Powell (2004) • Dey & Cruzvergara (2014) • Hayden & Ledwith (2014) • Smith (2014) • Nurmukhametov et al. (2015) • Mir (2016) • Kelkar (2016) • Young (2019)

system has been described in two different ways: (1) individual-oriented (interaction with the individual and their learning systems), and (2) Intrapersonal interactions (learner-learner, learner-instructor, learner-content-material/interface, etc.) that are both necessary during student life.

POSTGRADUATION STUDENT SUPPORT SERVICES

During this phase, students need services to help them find job opportunities. Student support services should be user-friendly and learner-centered; however, delivering effective and efficient service has always been a major challenge for higher education managers.

STUDENT SUPPORTIVE SERVICE DIMENSIONS

In the literature review, student support services include two types: academic and nonacademic services. The academic services are supervised by academic staff, are based on university decisions, and are related to teaching and learning issues and problems. However, nonacademic services are centralized services that are not related to the teaching-learning process but improve learning conditions (Tamulien?, 2014). Table 2 shows the attributes of each dimension.

SUPPORTIVE SERVICE PURPOSES

The purpose of student support is to increase graduation rates and improve student retention rates. There is competition between institutions to give grants. They also provide opportunities for students to improve their academic performance by motivating students. Supporting and enhancing the student experience from the first contact to becoming alumni is critical to success in higher education today for both the student and the institution. Student support and services contribute to the quality of students' learning experience and their academic success. Ciobanu said,

> The student services value needs greater recognition, support, and development in the interests of all students. Student services contribute to the quality of students' learning experience and their academic success, contribute as well at the university dropout rate decrease and to the increase in students' life diversity, encouraging and establishing an open method of making rational decisions and also resolving conflicts and preparing students for active involvement in society. (Ciobanu, 2013)

Table 3 shows the purposes of student supportive service.

DISCUSSION

Every day the higher education market is becoming more competitive. Many students are interested in online courses, and educational institutions need special program institutions to support students online to stay in the competition. Students seek to identify the best distance education program that can provide the most services and the quality of education (Allen & Seaman, 2010).

The result of extensive studies in this field show:

1. Student support is a general term used for institutions' wide range of services to help students complete their learning objectives and their course (Arko-Achemfuor, 2017).
2. Student support services are essential elements for all educational institutions, especially e-learning (Kumtepe et al., 2003).
3. Developing an organization-based support system is accomplished through techniques.
4. The primary focus of this support system is on the satisfaction and facilita-

Table 2. Dimensions of Student Supportive Service

Dimensions	References	Attributes
Academic services	• Farajollahi & Moenikia (2010) • Lee et al. (2013) • Stewart et al. (2013) • Newberry (2013) • Tamulienė (2014	A. Instructional services B. Registration of students C. Looking after admission D. Clear cut norms E. Preparation of guidelines and instructions F. Degree and transcript auditing G. Orientation courses H. Academic advising I. Course offering and availability J. Online representatives K. Learning material support L. Examination and evaluation services M. Tutoring services N. Ways of communication and interaction O. Online faculty advising P. Assignment help Q. Networking R. Contact tutoring S. Technical services T. Learning management system U. Learning content management system V. Infrastructure and facilities W. Library and bookstore services

Nonacademic services	• Pullan (2011)
	• Hunte (2012)
	• Noviyanti et al. (2018)
	• Gregori et al. (2018
	• Tuquero (2011)
		X. Counseling services
		   • Law consultations
		   • Academic counseling
		   • Health consultations
		   • Job counseling
		Y. General services
		   • Student help desk support
		   • Financial support
		   • Disability services
		   • Phone numbers
		   • Language training
		   • Information about distance learning opportunities
		   • Accommodation
		   • Social support services

Table 3. Purposes of Student Supportive Service

Definition (Purpose of Student Support Service)	References
Responsibility to the cognitive, affective, and social needs of students	• Nsamba & Makoe (2017)
Scientific success and removal of situational, organizational, and information barriers	• Sewart (1993) • Potter (1998) • Brindley (2014) • Rangara (2015)
Student engagement in the learning process	• McLoughlin (2002)

tion of learners (Cheawjindakarn et al., 2013).
5. The support for learners is an essential element in creating an effective learning experience for distance learning (Wright et al., 2013).
6. The support is the basis of an open learning system and can respond to the needs of the individual learning process (Thorpe, 2002).
7. In addition to studies focusing on the importance of learning support, the support of academic staff is necessary for the success of any distance education system (Gorder, 2008).

Floyd and Casey-Powell (2004) also reported that educational support creates a positive interactive environment between learners and staff. Various studies have shown that in successful universities worldwide, student support extends from pre-university to postgraduation (Ali et al., 2016; Astin & Vogelgesang, 2008; Athiyaman, 1997). Helping students develop and complete a professional resume and advising on interview strategies is needed. At some universities, such as Portland Community College, students can participate in different job workshops, such as how to succeed in job interviews, decision making, and goal setting. Rio Salado College also provides an electronic self-assessment tool and information on the job market in various occupations (Floyd & Casey-Powell, 2004).

Student support services are defined in two ways: academic and nonacademic services. Academic services are performed by academic staff and are based on university decisions related to teaching and learning issues and problems. However, nonacademic services are not related to academic topics, but they provide suitable conditions for the student (Räisänen & Fortanet-Gómez, 2008; Sewart, 1993; Tamulienė, 2014). Students' needs play an important role in designing and improving educational systems. Developing a quality management system in higher education is based on the student's expectations as customers, and evaluation of their opinions, especially in the negative ones, can improve quality (Eagle & Brennan, 2007; Kochhar, 1984). Student support services guarantee academic success. Student support services in the virtual environment are essential because in this space, the student feels alone (Shernoff, 2013). Teacher and student separation affects teaching and learning. A dynamic and active system helps students not to be isolated and decentralized. As a result, it prevents declining levels of motivation, interaction, and laziness (Jun, 2009). If supportive strategies are not considered in an e-learning system, there will be a rapid decline and an increase in dropout (Dalbani, 2009).

LIMITATIONS

First, the subdivision of dimensions was sometimes subjective and artificial. Secondly, we did not systematically evaluate the quality of the included research articles. Thirdly, the search was limited to articles that listed the search terms in their title. Finally, we only reviewed English articles.

CONCLUSION

Working in virtual education requires flexibility (Lenar et al., 2014). Some students leave online courses because they have low motivation and lack self-management skills. Student support services have emerged to overcome all these problems for the effective and sustainable distance education system (Chatpakkarattana & Khlaisang, 2013). The institution should provide face-to-face and distance support services.

The student support system can encourage students and faculty in cyberspace (Wagner et al., 2008). All individuals and structural resources in the distance education system should be considered an integral part of support services. Student support services in this type of education can create favorable conditions for the student. Unfortunately, even experienced virtual educational institutions are not paying attention to the student support system. Research in this area has been scant and has only focused on when the student support system should be activated (Adelman, 2009). No research has shown that supports fit the students' needs (Tamulienė, 2014).

Acknowledgments: This article is part of a research project approved by xxxx Medical Affairs Strategic Research Center (xxxxxx). We appreciate all the professors who collaborated on this research. The National Agency funded this project for Strategic Research in Medical Education. xxxxxx. xxxxxxx. Grant No.xxxxxxx. This research did not have any conflicts of interest with any individual or organization.

REFERENCES

Adelman, C. (2009). The Bologna Process for US eyes: Re-learning higher education in the age of convergence. *Institute for Higher Education Policy*. https://files.eric.ed.gov/fulltext/ED504904.pdf

Ali, F., Zhou, Y., Hussain, K., Nair, P. K., & Ragavan, N. A. (2016). Does higher education service quality affect student satisfaction, image, and loyalty? A study of international students in Malaysian public universities. *Quality Assurance in Education, 24*(1), 70–94. https://doi.org/10.1108/QAE-02-2014-0008

Allen, E., & Seaman, J. (2010). *Class differences: Online education in the United States, 2010*. Sloan Consortium.

Arko-Achemfuor, A. (2017). Student support gaps in an open distance learning context. *Issues in Educational Research, 27*(4), 658. http://www.iier.org.au/iier27/arko-achemfuor.html

Astin, A. W., Vogelgesang, L. J., & Ikeda, E. K. (1760). How service learning affects students. *Higher Education, 144*. https://digitalcommons.unomaha.edu/slcehighered/144

Athiyaman, A. (1997). Linking student satisfaction and service quality perceptions: The case of university education. *European Journal of Marketing, 31*(7), 528–540. https://doi.org/10.1108/03090569710176655

Brindley, J. E. (2014). Learner support in online distance education: Essential and evolving. *Online Distance Education. Towards a Research Agenda*, 287–310. http://cf2015.bhcarroll.edu/files/session-2-toward-a-learning-century

Chatpakkarattana, T., & Khlaisang, J. (2013). The learner support system for distance education. *Creative Education, 3*(8), 47. https://www.scirp.org/pdf/CE_2013011708304065.pdf

Cheawjindakarn, B., Suwannatthachote, P., & Theeraroungchaisri, A. (2013). Critical success factors for online distance learning in higher education: A review of the literature. *Creative Education, 3*(8), 61. https://www.scirp.org/html/26754.htm

Ciobanu, A. (2013). The role of student services in improving student experience in higher education. *Procedia-Social and Behavioral Sciences, 92*, 169–173. https://doi.org/10.1016/j.sbspro.2013.08.654

Dalbani, H. (2009). Autonomy in distance English language learning. *Damascus University Journal*, 1–26. http://new.damascusuniversity.edu.sy/mag/human/images/

Darojat, O., & Sunarsih, D. (2014). *Learner support services: Policies and Implementation at Universitas Terbuka, Indonesia*. https://xueshu.baidu.com/usercenter/paper/show?paperid

Dey, F., & Cruzvergara, C. Y. (2014). Evolution of career services in higher education. *New Directions for Student Services, 148*, 5–18. https://doi.org/10.1002/ss.20105

Duffy, F. D., & Holmboe, E. S. (2006). Self-assessment in lifelong learning and improving performance in practice: Physician know thyself. *Journal of the American Medical Association, 296*(9), 1137–1139. http://jama.ama-assn.org/cgi/content/full/296/9/1137

Eagle, L., & Brennan, R. (2007). Are students customers? TQM and marketing perspectives. *Quality Assurance in Education, 15*(1), 44–60. https://www.emerald.com/insight/content/doi/10.1108/0968488071

Farajollahi, M., & Moenikia, M. (2010). The study of relation between students support services and distance students' academic achievement. *Procedia-Social and Behavioral Sciences, 2*(2), 4451–4456. https://doi.org/10.1016/j.sbspro.2010.03.710

Floyd, D. L., & Casey-Powell, D. (2004). New roles for student support services in distance learning. *New Directions for Community Colleges, 128*, 55–64. https://doi.org/10.1002/cc.175

Frehywot, S., Vovides, Y., Talib, Z., Mikhail, N., Ross, H., Wohltjen, H., & Scott, J. (2013). E-learning in medical education in resource-constrained low-and middle-income countries. *Human Resources for Health, 11*(1), 4. http://www.human-resources-health.com/content/11/1/4

Gorder, L. M. (2008). A study of teacher perceptions of instructional technology integration in the classroom. *Delta Pi Epsilon Journal, 50*(2), 63–76. https://web.b.ebscohost.com/abstract?direct=true&profile

Gregori, E. B., Zhang, J., Galván-Fernández, C., & de Asís Fernández-Navarro, F. (2018). Learner support in MOOCs: Identifying variables linked to completion. *Computers & Education, 122*, 153–168. https://doi.org/10.1016/j.compedu.2018.03.014

Gujjar, A. A., Naoreen, B., & Chaudhry, A. H. (2010). A comparative study of student support services: The United Kingdom, Pakistan and Sri Lanka. *Procedia-Social and Behavioral Sciences, 2*(2), 839–846. https://doi.org/10.1016/j.sbspro.2010.03.113

Hayden, S. C., &Ledwith, K. E. (2014). Career services in university external relations. *New Directions for Student Services, 148*, 81–92. https://doi.org/10.1002/ss.20110

Hunte, S. (2012). First-time online learners' perceptions of support services provided. *Turkish Online Journal of Distance Education, 13*(2), 180–197. https://dergipark.org.tr/en/download/article-file/155918

Jain, P., Salooja, M., & Mythili, G. (2016). An analytical study of web support in distance education programmes. *Indian Journal of Open Learning, 25*(3), 187–203. https://www.learntechlib.org/p/187823/.

Jun, J. S. (2004). *Understanding the factors of adult learners dropping out of e-learning courses.* https://newprairiepress.org/cgi/viewcontent.cgi?article=2802&context=aerc

Kelkar, D. (2016). *Creating possibilities: An examination of university career support services for international students in British Columbia.* https://summit.sfu.ca/item/16300

Kochhar, S. K. (1984). *Guidance and counseling in colleges and universities*. Sterling.

Kumtepe, E. G., Toprak, E., Ozturk, A., Buyukkose, G. T., Kilinc, H., & Menderis, İ. A. (2003). *Support services in open and distance education: An integrated model of open universities.* https://https://members.aect.org/pdf/Proceedings/procee

LaPadula, M. (2003). A comprehensive look at online student support services for distance learners. *The American Journal of Distance Education, 17*(2), 119–128. https://doi.org/10.1207/S15389286AJDE1702_4

Lee, Y., Choi, J., & Kim, T. (2013). Discriminating factors between completers of and dropouts from online learning courses. *British Journal of Educational Technology, 44*(2), 328–337. https://doi.org/10.1111/j.1467-8535.2012.01306.x

Lehtinen, E., Hakkarainen, K., Lipponen, L., Rahikainen, M., &Muukkonen, H. (1999). Computer supported collaborative learning: A review. *The JHGI Giesbers Reports on Education, 10*. https://d1wqtxts1xzle7.cloudfront.net/40470387

Lenar, S., Artur, F., Ullubi, S., & Nailya, B. (2014). Problems and decisions in the field of distance education. *Procedia-Social and Behavioral Sciences, 131*, 111–117. https://doi.org/10.1016/j.sbspro.2014.04.088

Liu, Q., Hu, R., Zhan, X., & Yan, W. (2014, October). Evaluation of students' satisfaction and attitudes toward blended learning in medical education: A survey in randomized controlled trial course. In *European Conference on e-Learning* (p. 679). Academic Conferences International Limited.

Lopez-Catalan, B., & Bañuls, V. A. (2017). A Delphi-based approach for detecting key e-learning trends in post-graduate education. *Education+ Training, 59*(6), 590–604. http://www.emeraldinsight.com/0040-0912.htm

Lu, P., & Luo, L. (2017, February). An analysis of learning efficiency affecting factors in open education learners. In *2017 International Conference on Humanities Science, Management and Education Technology*. Atlantis Press. https://doi.org/10.2991/hsmet-17.2017.176

McKenna, H. (2006). *Nursing theories and models*. Routledge. https://doi.org/10.4324/9780203135440

McLoughlin, C. (2002). Learner support in distance and networked learning environments: Ten dimensions for successful design. *Distance Education, 23*(2), 149–162. https://doi.org/10.1080/0158791022000009178

Mir, K. (2017). Design and development of online student support system. *Distance Online Learn, 3*(1), 1–8. https://doi.org/10.1080/0158791022000009178

Morse, J. M., Hupcey, J. E., Mitcham, C., & Lenz, E. R. (1996). Concept analysis in nursing research: A critical appraisal. *Scholarly Inquiry for Nursing Practice, 10*(3), 253–277. https://doi.org/10.1891/0889-7182.10.3.253

Newberry, R. (2013). Building a foundation for success through student services for online learners. *Online Learning Journal, 17*(4). https://www.learntechlib.org/p/183761/

Noviyanti, M., Sudarwo, R., Mardiana, A., & Budima, M. H. (2018). The importance-performance analysis (IPA) on academic and non-academic services to enhance student motivation. *The Online Journal of Distance Education and e-Learning, 6*(1), 78. https://tojdel.net/journals/tojdel/volumes/tojdel-volume06-i01.pdf#page=85

Nsamba, A., & Makoe, M. (2017). Evaluating quality of students' support services in open distance learning. *Turkish Online Journal of Distance Education, 18*(4), 91–103. https://doi.org/10.17718/tojde.340391

Nurmukhametov, N., Temirova, A., & Bekzhanova, T. (2015). The problems of development of distance education in Kazakhstan. *Procedia-social and Behavioral Sciences, 182*, 15–19. https://doi.org/10.1016/j.sbspro.2015.04.729

Potter, J. (1998). Beyond access: Student perspectives on support service needs in distance learning. *Canadian Journal of University Continuing Education, 24*(1). https://doi.org/10.21225/D5R88Q

Pullan, M. (2011). Online support services for undergraduate millennial students. *Information Systems Education Journal, 9*(1), 67. http://isedj.org/2011-9/N1/ISEDJv9n1p67.html

Räisänen, C., & Fortanet-Gómez, I. (2008). The state of ESP teaching and learning in Western European higher education after Bologna. *ESP in European Higher Education: Integrating language and content, 4*, 11–51. https://doi.org/10.1075/aals.4.03rai

Rangara, T. A. (2015). Assessing learner support services rendered to undergraduate students at selected distance learning institutions [Doctoral dissertation, University of South Africa]. https://core.ac.uk/download/pdf/43178179.pdf

Sahoo, P. K. (2018). Unit 1: Learner support: A systems approach. IGNOU. http://www.egyankosh.ac.in/bitstream/123456789/41705/1/Unit-1.pdf

Sánchez-Elvira Paniagua, A., & Simpson, O. (2018). Developing student support for open and distance learning: The EMPOWER project. *Journal of Interactive Media in Education, 2018*(1). https://files.eric.ed.gov/fulltext/EJ1187910.pdf

Schwartz-Barcott, D., & Kim, H. S. (2000). An expansion and elaboration of the hybrid model of concept development. *Concept Development in Nursing, 26*(4), 129–159. https://ci.nii.ac.jp/naid/10026506850/

Sewart, D. (1993). Student support systems in distance education. *Open Learning: The Journal of Open, Distance and e-Learning, 8*(3), 3–12. https://doi.org/10.1080/0268051930080302

Shernoff, D. J. (2013). *Optimal learning environments to promote student engagement.* Springer.

Shieh, C. J., & Yu, L. (2016). A study on information technology integrated guided discovery instruction towards students' learning achievement and learning retention. *Eurasia Journal of Mathematics, Science & Technology Education, 12*(4), 833–842. https://doi.org/10.12973/eurasia.2015.1554a

Smith, K. K. (2014). Strategic directions for career services within the university setting [Special ed.]. *New Directions for Student Services, 148.* https://onlinelibrary.wiley.com/toc/15360695/2014/2014/148

Stewart, B. L., Goodson, C. E., Miertschin, S. L., Norwood, M. L., & Ezell, S. (2013). Online student support services: A case-based on quality frameworks. *Journal of Online Learning and Teaching, 9*(2), 290. https://www.researchgate.net/profile/Barbara-Stewart/publication/342364946

Tait, A. (2000). Planning student support for open and distance learning. *Open Learning: The Journal of Open, Distance and e-Learning, 15*(3), 287–299. https://doi.org/10.1080/713688410

Tamulienė, R. (2014). Adjusting college students' support services to students' type: Lithuania's case. *Procedia-Social and Behavioral Sciences*, *141*, 438–446. https://doi.org/10.1016/j.sbspro.2014.05.077

Thorpe, M. (2002). Rethinking learner support: The challenge of collaborative online learning. *Open Learning: The Journal of Open, Distance and e-Learning*, *17*(2), 105–119. https://doi.org/10.1080/02680510220146887a

Tuquero, J. M. (2011). A meta-ethnographic synthesis of support services in distance learning programs. *Journal of Information Technology Education*, *10*, 157–179. http://jite.informingscience.org/documents/Vol10/JITEv10IIPp157-179Tuquero974.pdf

Unwin, P. T. H., & Unwin, T. (Eds.). (2009). *ICT4D: Information and communication technology for development*. Cambridge University Press.

Usun, S. (2004). Factors affecting the application of information and communication technologies (ICT) in distance education. *Turkish Online Journal of Distance Education-TOJDE*, *5*(1). https://dergipark.org.tr/en/download/article-file/156515

Wagner, N., Hassanein, K., & Head, M. (2008). Who is responsible for e-learning success in higher education? A stakeholders' analysis. *Journal of Educational Technology & Society*, *11*(3), 26–36. https://www.jstor.org/stable/jeductechsoci.11.3.26

Walker, L. O., & Avant, K. C. (2005). *Strategies for theory construction in nursing*. http://catalogue.pearsoned.ca/assets/hip/ca/hip_ca_pearsonhighered/preface/0134754077.pdf

Wikipedia. (2019, December 14). Blended learning. https://en.wikipedia.org/w/index.php?title=Blended_learning&oldid=930674805

Wright, K. B., Rosenberg, J., Egbert, N., Ploeger, N. A., Bernard, D. R., & King, S. (2013). Communication competence, social support, and depression among college students: A model of Facebook and face-to-face support network influence. *Journal of Health Communication*, *18*(1), 41–57. https://doi.org/10.1080/10810730.2012.688250

Young, M. (2019). Career services: Roles beyond job seeking. *Education for Employability*, *2*, 179–188. https://doi.org/10.1163/9789004418707_015

Yukselturk, E., & Yildirim, Z. (2008). Investigation of interaction, online support, course structure, and flexibility as the contributing factors to students' satisfaction in an online certificate program. *Journal of Educational Technology & Society*, *11*(4), 51–65. https://www.jstor.org/stable/jeductechsoci.11.4.51

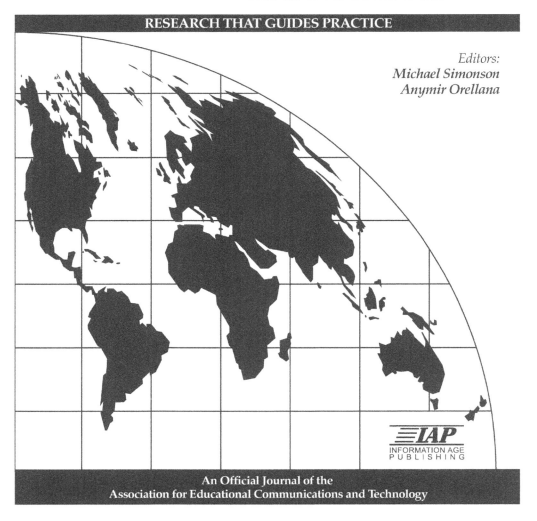

Students, Presentations, and the Pandemic
Restructuring Assignments and Assessment

Cheyenne Seymour

Public speaking is a concern for many students. Research has pointed to the professional benefits of honing oral communication skills despite the potential aversion to it. This article highlights how college students' speech apprehension and their need to communicate with audiences effectively have been impacted by the COVID-19 pandemic. In addition, I reflect on the first-hand practice of teaching communication courses to undergraduates during the pandemic, which required the delivery of presentations using learning management systems (LMS) and videoconferencing applications. Through efforts to restructure assignments and assessments, I was able to aid students in advancing their ability to communicate with virtual audiences.

Keywords: undergraduate, oral communication, distance learning, scaffolding, pandemic

Cheyenne Seymour,
EdD, Assistant Professor, City University of New York, Bronx Community College, 2155 University Avenue, Bronx, NY 10453.
Email: Cheyenne.Seymour@bcc.cuny.edu

INTRODUCTION

In the spring of 2020, educators were catapulted into the facilitation of distance learning due to the emergence of the COVID-19 pandemic and, in many cases, without being afforded the time and resources to fully prepare in advance. Out of necessity faculty, such as myself, adapted curriculum, assessment methods, and modes of teaching to achieve educational goals and prioritize the health and safety of our respective learning communities.

As part of assessment, I require college students in communication courses to deliver oral presentations, which allows them to demonstrate their content knowledge and ability to effectively impart information verbally and nonverbally. Before the pandemic, the undergraduates in my introductory-level public speaking and interpersonal communication courses would be asked to deliver presentations from a focal point in the classroom. However, the quick shift to distance learning required that I assign virtual presentations to students in online courses. The process of restructuring oral presentations to fit the online modality allowed students to deliver organized presentations with enhanced communication skills learned in the course. Examining my teaching practice and students' experience has led to identifying benefits and limitations.

LITERATURE REVIEW

Before the COVID-19 pandemic, many colleges and universities have created opportunities for students to learn remotely; some institutions offered individual courses online, while others ran fully remote degree programs. Educators have experimented with computers to facilitate learning since the late 1970s and early 1980s (Harting & Erthal, 2005). As technology has advanced, higher education institutions have adopted various forms of distance learning. Synchronous learning allows faculty and students to interact in a virtual classroom in real time, using conferencing techniques (McBrien et al., 2009). Asynchronous learning is not designed for real-time connection. Instead, it allows a learning community to access educational resources and complete coursework at independently selected time intervals. For many asynchronous courses, discussion boards are essential for engagement (Ringler et al., 2015). Discussion boards allow learning communities to exchange written messages and embed or link to other mediums, such as videos, audio clips, images, and more.

Another form of distance learning allows students and educators to combine elements of both synchronous and asynchronous modalities. Some educators know this format as the blended modality, which offers face-to-face and online learning (Garrison & Kanuka, 2004). The blended or hybrid model's in-person component can occur in the same physical setting or virtual learning spaces. Fully remote blended courses are designed with synchronous class meetings and asynchronous class discussions (Yamagata-Lynch, 2019).

Due to the pandemic, colleges and universities shifted to distance learning in the spring of 2020. This shift resulted in a collection of educators and students who both experienced and unfamiliar with remote teaching and learning, respectively. One international study found that faculty who previously instructed students online, taught in higher education, and facilitated learning using synchronous modalities showed the most engagement and ability to deal with the shift to distance learning due to the pandemic (Jelińska & Paradowski, 2021).

The fear of public speaking has been identified during adolescence and adult years (Comadena & Prusank, 1988; Rolls, 1998; van Dis et al., 2021; Vevea et al., 2009). This fear is also the experience of many college students, who worry about addressing public audiences (Dwyer & Davidson, 2012; Marinho et al., 2017). There are several causes of speech apprehension, and some students develop physical symptoms associated with their fear (Grieve et al., 2021; Smith et al., 2005).

When academic course work requires the oral delivery of assignments, students are challenged to tackle their fear of speaking to a group of listeners. Many students want to work on the craft of effective oral communication; one study found that just under 90% of undergraduates desired courses that aimed to improve their public speaking skills (Marinho et al., 2017).

When college students, preparing to enter the workforce, acquire the skills needed to communicate with remote professional audiences effectively, there are many benefits (Briant & Crowther, 2020; Wolverton & Tanner, 2019). One of such benefits is securing employment by succeeding in virtual interviews. Before the pandemic, virtual career fairs and interviews were on the rise (Kirkwood et al., 2011). After the start of the pandemic, in addition to meeting with job recruiters remotely, many professionals are working outside of brick-and-mortar office spaces. By the fall of 2020, more than 70% of employed adults were performing job duties remotely (Pew Research Center, 2020). For many working professionals, it is essential to obtain communication skills that allow for clear and concise messaging with internal colleagues and external audiences, such as clients or customers.

Researchers have found that one of the top skills that convey a candidate's job readiness is speech communication (Baird & Parayitam, 2019; Stevens, 2005). When students can first develop effective oral communication skills in an educational setting and later demonstrate them in job interviews, they enhance their chance of securing employment.

APPROACH TO INQUIRY

This inquiry aimed to determine if undergraduates, who were required to deliver oral presentations to remote audiences, would succeed in conveying organized content with effective verbal and nonverbal communication skills, following the required shift to distance learning. Due to the pandemic, my courses in the latter half of spring 2020, fall 2020, spring 2021, and summer 2021 were all online. Over this period, I taught ($N = 214$) students in 11 sections of interpersonal communication and public speaking to community college students in the northeast. Two sections switched to an asynchronous modality in March of 2020. The subsequent semesters were taught online for the full duration; seven sections were taught asynchronously, and two were taught synchronously. Students were required to deliver one oral presentation in interpersonal communication, and those enrolled in public speaking were required to deliver three presentations of varying type.

To effectively help students strengthen their oral communication skills and confidently navigate the technology required for virtual presentations, I took two approaches, including teaching the students about the applications they would be required to use for delivery and scaffolding the assignments.

Before students delivered a formal presentation, I first developed and shared guides on using the required application(s). I followed that with simple, low-stakes assignments or activities that allowed my students to utilize the basic application functions required to later deliver presentations. For example, students in asynchronous classes gained experience by first recording themselves sharing their presentation topic and summarizing the sources of research that they planned to incorporate. Similarly, students in synchronous online courses summarized their topics and resources, but on screen in real time.

SCAFFOLDING ASSIGNMENTS

To ensure that all low-stakes assignments successfully complimented upcoming formal presentations, students were to identify one visual, audio, or audiovisual that they intended to feature in an upcoming presentation. They practiced sharing their presentational aid with a virtual audience to gain familiarity with the functions of the platform they would soon use to impart their content knowledge.

Through scaffolding, in courses that met in real time on camera, I provided students with the experience of sharing messages both synchronously and asynchronously as preparation for formal presentations. This experience provided them with insight on the virtual modality that felt most comfortable, helped them to sharpen their technological skills, and allowed them to identify any challenges that they could encounter based on the device, audio equipment (headsets and microphones), or internet connection they had while working remotely.

RESULTS

About 62% of students expressed a fear of public speaking. Those who shared their apprehension cited various causes. These reasons include previous negative experiences, a fear of not looking one's best on camera, having presentations shared on social media sites without consent, misspeaking, and talking to an audience in a non-native language. The most reoccurring concern was that students worried about being judged by others.

Students also experienced technical problems. Twenty-four percent of students encountered at least one problem as they attempted to share presentations with their academic audience; some problems were self-reported. Others were identified when there was difficulty accessing the student's presentation. The cause of students' technological challenges includes limited access to devices due to sharing a single computer with multiple members of a household, the inability to record a large video file on a device with limited storage capacity, owning a mobile device that was incompatible with applications required for the completion of assignments, and difficulty navigating the learning management system (LMS). Issues with Wi-Fi also stifled the completion of some presentations, which resulted in out-of-sync audio as students attempted to address audiences in real time. Students in asynchronous classes reported the inability to upload large video files due to weak and unavailable Wi-Fi signals.

Those enrolled in asynchronous courses expressed an appreciation for being able to re-record their presentations to their satisfaction. Forty-seven percent saw this as an opportunity to maximize their ability to meet the requirements of an assignment. However, the downside was that this added advantage led to an increased amount of time devoted to a single presentation.

Teaching communication courses online to undergraduates, while utilizing virtual presentations as one assessment method, led me to identify three areas that required careful consideration to help students effectively address virtual audiences.

When assigning student presentations, I first had to consider which platform would be optimal for sharing. The platform I used for asynchronous courses was Blackboard, the college provided LMS. My students' familiarity with Blackboard, prior to the pandemic, was a key factor in this choice. Blackboard allows faculty to set up assessments where a student's recorded presentation can be accessed by the instructor or by classmates. As an educator, I find it imperative that students in asynchronous courses share their presentations with classmates to receive constructive feedback from peers, just as they would in a campus classroom, so I requested that students submit their recordings to the discussion board. Sharing ignited engagement regarding the subject matter of the presentations and the students' oral communication skills. For students who experienced technical difficulty uploading large video files to Blackboard directly, I suggested YouTube as a vehicle for sharing. I found that many students appreciated the reduced upload times on YouTube compared to the LMS. Students would then share the YouTube link or embed the video in Blackboard. When teaching two synchronous courses, I taught one with the LMS and the second with a combination of the LMS and a videoconferencing platform. Using Blackboard's Collaborate Ultra tool in one course, my students and I could appear on screen in real time while using a single application for all coursework. In the second synchronous course, I chose Zoom for student presentations. While

Zoom and Blackboard Collaborate Ultra functioned primarily the same by allowing users to meet in real time and share presentational aids, Zoom offered individuals an option to alter their background by blurring or replacing it with an alternate visual, which afforded privacy to students as they worked remotely. However, since Zoom did not function like an LMS, I also required the use of Blackboard for the submission of all other academic work.

Furthermore, there were reasons that I opted not to use other available video-sharing applications in synchronous courses. Although YouTube offered users the ability to share in a live mode, this video-sharing and social media site presented challenges for a community of learners in a synchronous course. This challenge was because I, as the instructor, could not moderate when needed. Instead, only the person speaking in real time on their YouTube channel could share a message. Attempting to hear from multiple student speakers in one class period would require navigating from one YouTube channel to the next, using only one-way communication, so I did not conduct class using this platform.

Some textbook publishers have recognized a need for students to capture and share oral presentations in recent years. Some have developed software that enable students to share live or prerecorded presentations. I have used a publisher-provided sharing platform before the pandemic; I found the array of grading options, which allowed faculty to align commentary with specific parts of a recording or provide general feedback to be helpful. However, using these features required faculty to select supplemental packages when adopting the textbook prior to the start of the semester, and this feature is not available for all texts.

The second area that required careful consideration was the rubric used for assessment. I altered the rubrics used for in-person delivery to grade virtual presentations. I took this approach because while the physical classroom allowed for equitable use of space and technology, there were inconsistencies with these criteria when students recorded or presented live off-campus. When students delivered an assigned speech in a classroom, I had a full view of their nonverbal communication while assessing their efforts, but this was not always the case in a virtual presentation due to the type of recording device and placement of the camera. Students with a supplemental mounted webcam were able to adjust the angle in a way that one relying on a tablet could not, due to the design of devices. At a minimum, I was able to see a portion of the speaker through a headshot or bust shot, which highlighted an area above the abdomen to the top of a speaker's head and limited the view of gestures. I was also keenly aware that requiring students to present while standing in full view of the camera could result in low volume, as speakers move away from their devices to offer audiences a wide or medium-wide shot. Therefore, I had to consider the way volume was assessed. While volume is an important component to consider when grading a student presentation, the use of devices and microphones could drastically impact the quality of audio. Students who recorded presentations for asynchronous courses could potentially use video editing software to raise the naturally captured volume. At the same time, those delivering live presentations in synchronous classes needed to troubleshoot the audio levels to sync their equipment to the platform or move closer to the microphone to ensure clear audio.

Furthermore, I revised the rubric to reflect what it means to establish eye contact with a virtual audience. Moving one's head from right to left periodically in a virtual presentation is ineffective, unlike when speaking to an audience face to face. Instead, I assessed students' ability to look into the camera's lens to connect with virtual viewers. In addition, I had to adapt rubrics when students were required or encouraged to use presentational aids. Doing so allowed me to compensate for the obstacles that may be out of a student's control when delivering virtual presentations and displaying objects, sharing audiovisuals, or using other supplemental items. For example, if a speaker held an item with writing up to the camera, the words were inverted from the audience's perspective. Also, since many of the videoconferencing applications have nuances, I had to consider this while assessing student work. When slideshows were shared in Blackboard Collaborate Ultra, the virtual audience could advance slides, whether intended or unintended by clicking another slide. While screen sharing in Zoom, audiences could have an obstructed view of the presenter's screen depending upon settings and a secondary application tool, like the chat box. Therefore, I remained available throughout the semester to aid students with navigating ways to optimize their performance with their devices and applications.

The third area that required thoughtful consideration was student privacy. The recording and virtual sharing of presentations with an entire class was not something I could avoid while teaching a communication course. So instead, I approached it mindfully. Some students could feel uncomfortable that classmates could access their likeness and academic efforts with a few clicks on a device. As faculty, I felt it was important to empower students to make decisions about access to their work. In part, this was done by requesting consent to record student presentations in synchronous classes. If students did not grant consent, I solely relied on taking notes on presentations in real time, like the process I used in campus classrooms. For students sharing their presentations in an asynchronous format, I recommended that students who opted to upload their videos to YouTube, opposed to the LMS directly, used the "unlisted" feature, which allowed only those with the URL to access the content. Furthermore, to empower students, I announced that they could remove content from a sharing platform after the assessment was graded. Although many students belong to the demographic known as digital natives, due to the lifelong use of digital technology, empowering students allowed me to give them control over digital access to their work and create a supportive and respectful learning environment.

Conclusion

The students in my online courses delivered organized presentations while demonstrating content knowledge and effective verbal and nonverbal communication skills. However, to achieve this objective, students had to confront the fear of public speaking. While the COVID-19 pandemic may have changed the educational landscape, it did not change the likelihood that students can experience apprehension involving public speaking. The pressure to deliver content confidently while navigating technology skillfully has added to the gravity of the assessment for many students. Scaffolding assignments allowed my students to gradually build the knowledge and confidence needed to develop effective oral communication skills, which will help them achieve both their academic and professional goals.

Several variables are involved in preparing and delivering student presentations in online courses. The modality of distance learning (synchronous or asynchronous), LMS, video-sharing applications, individual recording devices, and Internet quality can create unique obstacles for educators and students. In some areas of the United States, Wi-Fi connections have been unreliable during the pandemic, and receiving equipment to provide access was delayed (Khazan, 2020; Richards et al., 2021). Locations with weak Wi-Fi signals have been barriers for students who attempted to deliver live presentations due to image distortions and poorly synced audio. Weak signals have also impeded the progress of uploading an asynchronous recording to the LMS or video sharing site. With pre-planning and consideration of potential obstacles, faculty can help mitigate challenges by identifying how to best utilize the LMS to deliver presentations. Considering the mode of instruction can help with the decision to incorporate the use of additional applications and video sharing sites.

Although challenges exist for faculty and students, when assessment requires the delivery of oral presentations online, undergraduates are gaining valuable experience that will help them to succeed in the modern-day workplace. Learning to complement organized information with body language and vocal technique will help students achieve academic success in subsequent academic courses and enter the workplace ready to adapt to various communication channels and modalities.

REFERENCES

Baird, A. M., & Parayitam, S. (2019). Employers' ratings of importance of skills and competencies college graduates need to get hired: Evidence from the New England region of USA. *Education& Training*, 61(5), 622–634. http://doi.org/10.1108/ET-12-2018-0250

Briant, S., & Crowther, P. (2020). Reimagining internships through online experiences: Multidisciplinary engagement for creative industries students. *International Journal of Work-Integrated Learning*, 21(5), 617–628.

Comadena, M. E., & Prusank, D. T. (1988). Communication apprehension and academic achievement among elementary and middle school students. *Communication Education*, 37(4), 270–277. https://doi.org/10.1080/03634528809378728

Dwyer, K., & Davidson, M. (2012). Is public speaking really more feared than death? *Communication Research Reports*, 29(2), 99–107. https://doi.org/10.1080/08824096.2012.667772

Garrison, D. R., & Kanuka, H. (2004). Blended learning: Uncovering its transformative potential in higher education. *The Internet and Higher Education*, 7(2), 95–105. https://doi.org/10.1016/j.iheduc.2004.02.001

Grieve, R., Woodley, J., Hunt, S. E., & McKay, A. (2021). Student fears of oral presentations and public speaking in higher education: A qualitative survey. *Journal of Further & Higher Education*, 1–13. https://doi.org/10.1080/0309877x.2021.1948509

Harting, K., & Erthal, M. J. (2005). History of distance learning. *Information Technology, Learning, and Performance Journal*, 23(1), 35–44.

Jelińska, M., & Paradowski, M. B. (2021). Teachers' engagement in and coping with emergency remote instruction during COVID-19-induced school closures: A multinational contextual perspective. *Online Learning Journal*, 25(1), 303–328. https://doi.org/10.24059/olj.v25i1.2492

Khazam, O. (2020, August 17). America's terrible internet is making quarantine worse. *The Atlantic*. https://www.theatlantic.com/technology/archive/2020/08/virtual-learning-when-you-dont-have-internet/615322/

Kirkwood, J., Gutgold, N. D., & Manley, D. (2011). Hello world, it's me: Bringing the basic speech communication course into the digital age. *Communication Teacher*, 25(3), 150–153. https://doi.org/10.1080/17404622.2011.579905

Marinho, A. C. F., de Medeiros, A. M., Gama, A. C. C., & Teixeira, L. C. (2017). Fear of public speaking: Perception of college students and correlates. *Journal of Voice*, 31(1), e7–e11. https://doi.org/10.1016/j.jvoice.2015.12.012

McBrien, J. L., Cheng, R. & Jones, P. (2009). Virtual spaces: Employing a synchronous online classroom to facilitate student engagement in online learning. *International Review of Research in Open and Distributed Learning*, 10(3). https://doi.org/10.19173/irrodl.v10i3.605

Pew Research Center. (2020). How the coronavirus outbreak has—And hasn't—Changed the way Americans work. https://www.pewresearch.org/social-trends/2020/12/09/how-the-coronavirus-outbreak-has-and-hasnt-changed-the-way-americans-work/

Richards, E., Aspegren, E., & Mansfield, E. (2021, February 4). A year into the pandemic, thousands of students still can't get reliable

Wi-Fi for school. The digital divide remains worse than ever. *USA Today*. https://www.usatoday.com/story/news/education/2021/02/04/covid-online-school-broadband-internet-laptops/3930744001/

Ringler, I., Schubert, C., Deem, J., Flores, J., Friestad-Tate, J., & Lockwood, R. (2015). Improving the asynchronous online learning environment using discussion boards. *Journal of Educational Technology*, *12*(1), 15–27.

Rolls, J. A. (1998). Facing the fears associated with professional speaking. *Business Communication Quarterly*, *61*(2), 103–106. https://doi.org/10.1177/108056999806100213

Smith, C. D., Sawyer, C. R., & Behnke, R. R. (2005). Physical symptoms of discomfort associated with worry about giving a public speech. *Communication Reports*, *18*(1-2), 31–41. https://doi.org/10.1080/08934210500084206

Stevens, B. (2005). What communication skills do employers want? Silicon Valley recruiters respond. *Journal of Employment Counseling*, *42*(1), 2–9. https://doi.org/10.1002/j.2161-1920.2005.tb00893.x

van Dis, E. A. M., Landkroon, E., Hagenaars, M. A., van der Does, F. H. S., & Engelhard, I. M. (2021). Old fears die hard: Return of public speaking fear in a virtual reality procedure. *Behavior Therapy*, *52*(5), 1188–1197. https://doi.org/10.1016/j.beth.2021.01.005

Vevea, N. N., Pearson, J. C., Child, J. T., & Semlak, J. L. (2009). The only thing to fear is … public speaking?: Exploring predictors of communication in the public speaking classroom. *Journal of the Communication, Speech & Theatre Association of North Dakota*, *22*, 1–8.

Wolverton, C. C., & Tanner, J. (2019). Teaching public speaking to business students in the digital age: Updating our methods. *International Journal of Education & Development Using Information Communication Technology*, *15*(3), 22–33.

Yamagata-Lynch, L. C. (2014). Blending online asynchronous and synchronous learning. *The International Review of Research in Open and Distributed Learning*, *15*(2), https://doi.org/10.19173/irrodl.v15i2.1778

Smile, Wink, Laugh

Incorporating Emojis to Increase Students' Perception of Instructor Humanness in an Online Spanish Course

Shelly Wyatt and María T. Redmon

INTRODUCTION

The benefits of online learning at the college and university level have been widely acknowledged, including improved writing and computer skills, anonymity that benefits students who are reluctant to participate in the physical classroom, increased course selection, and the ability to complete assignments when it is most convenient for individual students (Appana, 2008; Aslanian & Clinefelter, 2013; Daymont et al., 2011; Heap, 2017). Online degree programs designed to attract and meet the educational needs of adult learners rely heavily on computer technology; currently, there is no alternative approach that can reach so many students (Bart, 2016; Rodriquez & Nash, 2004). There is an investment on the part of the student, the instructor, and the institution; students must learn how to use the learning management system (LMS) and understand the design of the online

Shelly Wyatt,
PhD, Associate Instructional Designer,
University of Central Florida,
12351 Research Parkway, P.O. Box 162811,
Room 230A-X, Orlando, FL 32826-2811.

María T. Redmon,
MA, Senior Instructor, Modern Languages
and Literatures, Trevor Coburn Hall,
4000 Central Florida Blvd.,
Orlando, FL 32816.

course (Cole et al., 2017). While the benefits of online learning are substantial, there are also challenges: the tools that make online learning possible—the laptops, tablets, and smartphones—also constitute a digital barrier that limits instructor and learner communications to characters on a screen or grades in an online grade book. Online learning can feel very isolating and lonely because of the lack of contact with classmates and instructors (Bart, 2016). Although the newest LMSs incorporate more media and interactive elements than previous systems, online learning environments continue to rely heavily on text-based resources and communications that limit incorporating emotional context (Sarsar, 2017). However, it is the human element that still counts and may be the most challenging element of learning online: "We learned that instructional technology may be a way of enhancing and increasing learning opportunities, but in the end, the human factor matters most of all" (Rodriquez & Nash, 2004, p. 74). The human element in online learning, for this study, consists of the instructor incorporating ideograms, in the form of emojis, into online course discussions to add emotional context.

BACKGROUND OF THE STUDY

The reality of effective teaching in the online classroom involves being emotionally and cognitively present without the benefit of a physical presence. Students' perceived lack of an instructor presence in online courses has been associated with their expressed preference for face-to-face classes; some students associate online classes with learning entirely on their own, without the support of classmates and, more importantly, without an instructor (Delaney et al., 2010; Diebel & Grow, 2009; Tichavsky et al., 2015). "Students believe they would have to teach themselves or prefer a course taught by a 'human' or a 'real' teacher" (Tichavsky et al., 2015, p. 6).

More specifically, students' perception that their online course is managed automatically via an LMS leads to a belief that there is no one to whom they can turn for help, answer questions, or care about their performance in the course. Also, students have expressed the view that online courses are more challenging than face-to-face courses because of these missing elements that only an instructor can provide: their enthusiasm for the discipline, their ability to convey what is most important about the course topic, and their distinct personality (Tichavsky et al., 2015).

To be present in an online learning environment involves putting aside the false notion that an instructor can effectively hide behind a computer interface or that, at the very least, one is invisible. For most faculty teaching today, many of their experiences as students and new faculty have been rooted in the physical classroom, with bright lines that separate shared student-instructor spaces (classrooms, office hours, dining hall) from instructor-only spaces (office, home). The instructor's physical presence meant standing in front of neat rows of desks or at the head of a lecture hall; no extra effort was necessary to convey presence on the part of the instructor beyond simply showing up (McQuiggan, 2012). Because these physical student-instructor spaces do not exist in online classes, "some faculty simply put their lectures online and call it teaching" (McQuiggan, 2012, p. 32).

However, effective online teaching involves responding to students individually via email, online discussions, and online course chats; these communications are the core of online course management and serve to maintain course continuity (Conceição, 2006). While necessary, these interactions are not sufficient to convey the presence of an instructor in an online course; presence is a function not of transactions but space, even if that space is digital. Consistent with this line of thinking, an online instructor demonstrates presence "in the shape of an avatar [expressed as] a text, icon, image, or a three-dimensional shape; a teacher's digital body is a way of teaching and showing presence in an online setting" (Bolldén, 2016, p. 2).

THEORETICAL FRAMEWORK

The notion of social presence was introduced by Short et al. (1976), researchers in the field of social communications; they defined social presence as "the degree of salience of the other person in a mediated communication and the consequent salience of their interpersonal interactions" (p. 65). The contextualization of instructional communication using nonverbal cues was identified by Anderson (1979) as teacher nonverbal immediacy. These cues consist of eye contact, body language, facial expressions, gestures, appropriate touching, classroom space, and vocal expression: inflection, pitch, tone, pace (Kerssen-Griep & Witt, 2012).

In response to the rise of the digital world, Walther (1992) discovered that participants in online environments created visual interpretations of fellow participants based on their digital contributions to create a sense of closeness and identification. Gunawardena and Zittle (1997) helped shape the notion of online social presence by extending it to include the participants' feeling that they are interacting with a *real* person (Cunningham, 2015; Sung & Mayer, 2012).

The online teaching environment creates a new environment that is distinct from the onsite teaching environment; the presence of the instructor and the other students creates a learning space that neutralizes feelings of isolation and promotes a conducive learning environment (Bolldén, 2016; Lehman & Conceição, 2010). Still, the importance of social presence is not always clear to even experienced online instructors (Casey & Kroth, 2013). Social presence has been directly and indirectly linked to student satisfaction (Leong, 2011; Mathieson & Leafman, 2014). Social presence is a quality that students value in their online instructors (Akyol & Garrison, 2008; Caspi & Blau, 2008; Gunawardena & Zittle, 1997; Mathieson & Leafman, 2014).

Conversely, a lack of instructor social presence in an online course has been associated with student dissatisfaction, "an unreasonably critical attitude toward the instructor's effectiveness, and a lower level of affective learning" (Wei et al., 2012, p. 529). Bayne's (2005) study of identity construction in online learning environments found that teachers did not create an online social presence as much as constructing an identity rooted in control and authority. Not surprisingly, online educators have been strongly encouraged to consider social presence when designing and developing their online courses (Kear et al., 2014; Lee & Huang, 2018; Muilenburg & Berge, 2005).

Social presence is one of the three core elements of Garrison et al. (2000, 2003) community of inquiry framework, along with teaching presence and cognitive presence, and represents the "human third of the [community of inquiry] equation" (Mathieson & Leafman, 2014, p. 3). The founding concept of the community of inquiry framework is the vital role that community plays in effective online learning: "Within our model, we define social presence as the ability of learners to project themselves as 'real' people in a community of inquiry" (Garrison et al., 2003, p. 115). Social presence is rooted in social communication, or communication that is not directly related to the academic content; social communication conveys the following: humor, emotion, self-disclosure, appreciation, encouragement, and the acknowledgment of students as individuals (e.g., the use of names and nicknames; Garrison et al., 2010). Although the concepts of "teaching presence" and "social presence" may appear to describe the same phenomenon, teaching presence focuses specifically on students' perception of course content-related communications as well as course direction (Cole et al., 2017).

TOOLS OF HUMANIZATION: COMMUNICATION IN ONLINE CLASSES

The term LMS was developed initially in association with the PLATO K–12 learning system and described the course management component and not the content element (R. Foshay, personal communication, October 24, 2006, cited in Watson & Watson, 2007). According to Watson and Watson (2007), an LMS is defined as follows:

> [An] LMS is the framework that handles all the aspects of the learning process. An LMS is the infrastructure that delivers and manages instructional content, identifies and assesses individual and organizational learning or training goals, tracks the progress towards meeting those goals and collects and presents data for supervising the learning process of an organization as a whole. (p. 29)

Despite students' insistence that social presence is important to their learning, the design of LMSs has not focused on supporting the social presence of instructors in online courses (Kumar et al., 2011; Mathieson & Leafman, 2014). In an online course environment, social presence must be purposefully created and is not generated automatically as a function of the system itself. When teaching online, the traditional onsite classroom environment is not re-created; instead, an entirely new environment is created. The presence of other learners and the instructor is vital to facilitate a successful learning environment and avoid feelings of isolation (Lehman & Conceição, 2010).

EMOJIS

Emojis are small images that provide an emotional context for textual communication, often but not always on a mobile Internet-enabled device; they qualify as ideograms to represent an object, idea, or emotion without expressing its pronunciation. First introduced by Shigetaka Kurita in Japan in the late 1990s, these small pictures add emotional context and contextual cues to text-based communications on a mobile Internet-enabled device. The term "emoji" is derived from the Japanese characters for "picture" and "character," although it does evoke the English word for emotion (Skiba, 2016).

The term "emoji" is often used interchangeably with the term "emoticon," but they are not the same; emoticons are created by combining keyboard symbols to make pictures (e.g., <3 to represent a heart; Alshenqeeti, 2016). The smiley, formed by stringing together a colon, a dash, and a right parenthesis, is not a new invention. Harvey Ross Ball, an American graphic artist, invented the smiley in 1964 as part of an insurance company's efforts to raise employee morale by having the staff wear buttons with the smiley (Danesi, 2016). Not all emojis convey human emotion or experience: nonface emojis are more accurately called pictograms (e.g., a pizza emoji or a dog emoji; Riordan, 2017). Emojis were adopted with enthusiasm by Japanese users of mobile devices to convey emotional context and other information. The immense popularity of emojis and their ease of use and low cost transformed text-based messaging with its humor, sarcasm, affection, playfulness, and human feeling (Alshenqeeti, 2016; McIntyre, 2016; Moschini, 2016).

Used individually or strung together to create a more complex message, emojis add creativity that is an expression of the user (Tauch & Kanio, 2016). The power of emojis also lies in its universal nature, allowing users to bridge language and generational divides. In 2010, Google and Apple standardized over 722 emoji codes using the Unicode Consortium, and in 2011 Apple added an emoji keyboard to its operating system (iOS; Alshenqeeti, 2016; Doiron, 2018).

For current undergraduates of traditional or near-traditional college age (18–30), emojis are routinely included in their online communications and constitute 38% of users who send several messages with emojis on any given day (Emoji Research Team, 2016). These students have always been able to convey feelings and emotions with a few clicks on a keyboard; users of all ages in the digital world have made it clear that the emotional context of messages is important. Moreover, the context is more than just black and white, happy or sad: anger, sadness, confusion, relief, joy, and surprise are just some of the emojis that represent emotional context (Alshenqeeti, 2016). For instructors who wish to incorporate emojis into the course-related digital communications, Doiron (2018) suggests that the meaning or concept associated with a specific emoji be made clear to students: "an emoji lexicon for higher education needs to be created," and instructors should "include a lexicon in the course syllabus and provide examples of their use" (p. 8).

The universal nature of emojis is often noted and their potential to facilitate communication between individuals who do not share a common verbal language (Alshenqeeti, 2016; Gulsen, 2016). Although they are a relatively recent invention, early research indicates that emoticons/emojis can provide emotional context that clarifies the intended message behind digital communications (Kaye et al., 2016), take the place of non-verbal communications (Yuasa et al., 2011), and reveal the personality of the user (Wall et al., 2016). However, there is a potential for confusion because of differing platforms (e.g., Apple, Google, Twitter, Facebook) and cultural interpretations (Doiron, 2018; Miller et al., 2016).

Emojis' expression of emotion allows the instructor to create a digital persona (or e-persona) that extends their personality into the otherwise impersonal digital sphere (Clark, 1994; de Kerckhove & de Almeida, 2013). This capacity to convey personality may be associated with the emojis' because emojis come in various subjects, including universal facial expressions (Azuma, 2012). "In effect, they act as nonverbal surrogates, telling the reader what the writer's expression would be, and delivering additional social cues to support understanding of the message" (Alshenqeeti, 2016, p. 60).

OBJECTIVES AND HYPOTHESIS

Our objective is to present the concept of h-learning, a variation on the term e-learning, as it applies to digital communications and the humanizing effect of ideograms and other online course communication tools utilized at the University of Central Florida. This study aims to determine the impact of using emojis in online discussions on students' perception of the instructor's human presence.

> **Hypothesis 1:** Using emojis in online discussions will increase students' perception of the online instructor's human presence.

METHODOLOGY

This exploratory, quasi-experimental study took place at the University of Central Florida in Orlando, Florida, in the Department of Modern Languages and Literatures. The type of quasi-experimental design used in this study qualifies as a non-equivalent comparison group design; this design is widely used in educational research that involves an experimental and comparison group and a pretest and posttest (Campbell & Stanley, 1963). Students in two sections of an introductory Spanish language course (taught by the same instructor) served as the population, and participation in this study was voluntary. The Spanish language course was SPN1120C-Elementary Spanish Language, and Civilization I. Offered in both fall and spring semesters, SPN1120C "introduces the student to Spanish cul-

Please rate your impression of the instructor on these scales:

Fake	1	2	3	4	5	Natural
Machinelike	1	2	3	4	5	Humanlike
Artificial	1	2	3	4	5	Lifelike
Unkind	1	2	3	4	5	Kind
Apathetic	1	2	3	4	5	Responsive
Silent	1	2	3	4	5	Interactive
Unfriendly	1	2	3	4	5	Friendly
Dislike	1	2	3	4	5	Like
Uncaring	1	2	3	4	5	Caring
Unpleasant	1	2	3	4	5	Pleasant
Awful	1	2	3	4	5	Nice
Incompetent	1	2	3	4	5	Competent
Unengaged	1	2	3	4	5	Engaged
Absent	1	2	3	4	5	Present

Note: Adapted from "Godspeed" survey developed by Bartneck et al. (2019).

Figure 1. Survey measuring students' perception of instructor "humanness."

ture through the major language skills: listening, speaking, reading, and writing. Open only to students with no experience in this language" (University of Central Florida, 2018).

The instrument used to collect data from study participants (Figure 1) was adapted from a series of short surveys titled "Godspeed" (Appendix B); according to the authors of these surveys, the name "Godspeed" was selected because the intended audience was developers of robots. According to the authors Bartneck et al. (2009), the instrument was developed "for the technical developers of interactive robots who want to evaluate their creations without having to take a degree in experimental psychology" (p. 71).

The original purpose of this instrument was to standardize the measurement of human-robot interaction (HRI) by focusing on five HRI concepts: anthropomorphism, animacy, likeability, perceived intelligence, and perceived safety (Bartneck et al., 2009; Table 1). Although developed for evaluating interactive robots, the Godspeed series has been previously adapted for use in a study that focused on students' perceptions of the instructor through her digital feedback (Clark-Gordon et al., 2018).

The Cronbach's Alpha's for the questions in each concept (Table 1) were

Table 1. Five HRI Concepts to Measure
Human-Robot Interaction and Their Associated Questions

HRI Factors	Description of Factor	Questions in Godspeed Surveys	Questions in Adapted Godspeed Survey
Anthropomorphism	• The attribution of human characteristics, form, or behavior to a nonhuman object, such as animals, computers, or robots	• Fake/natural • Machinelike/humanlike • Unconscious/conscious • Artificial/lifelike • Moving rigidly/moving elegantly	• Fake/natural • Machinelike/humanlike • Artificial/lifelike
Animacy	• The characteristic of being lifelike; the perception of life	• Dead/alive • Stagnant/lively • Mechanical/organic • Artificial/lifelike • Inert/interactive • Apathetic/responsive	• Apathetic/Responsive • Silent/interactive • Engaged/unengaged • Absent/present
Likability	• The association of an individual with positive impressions, especially first impressions	• Nice/awful • Friendly/unfriendly • Kind/unkind • Pleasant/unpleasant	• Kind/unkind • Friendly/unfriendly • Dislike/like • Caring/uncaring • Unpleasant/pleasant • Awful/nice
Perceived intelligence	• The association of intelligence with a living creature	• Incompetent/competent • Ignorant/knowledgeable • Irresponsible/responsible • Unintelligent/intelligent • Foolish/sensible	• Incompetent/competent
Perceived safety	• The perception of danger associated with any interaction or situation	• Anxious/relaxed • Agitated/calm • Quiescent/surprised	

Source: Adapted from Bartneck et al. (2009).

reported by Bartneck et al. (2009) to be above 0.7, thus determining that the questionnaire has sufficient internal consistency reliability.

PROCEDURES

An exploratory study was conducted to identify which emojis to use as part of the experimental treatment to determine perceived emoji valence (Clark-Gordon et al., 2018). Unicode emojis (version 11.0) were used in this pilot study; they appear, with their potential meanings, in Table 2 (Full Emoji List, v11.0 2018).

To determine if the use of emojis by the instructor had an impact on students' perception of her human qualities, the instructor added emojis to her responses to students' online discussion posts (added as an image in the Canvas LMS; Figure 2). The number of online discussions was three and involved discussion of writing assignments. The pretest and posttest for each group (treatment and comparison) were administered through the Canvas LMS using the Quiz (graded anonymous survey) function that allows respondents to remain anonymous while still earning extra credit points as an

Table 2. Unicode Emojis Included in Pilot Test

Emojis	Potential Meanings
😃	Big smile
😆	Laughing
😉	Winking
🤔	Thinking
🙂	Smile
🤗	Clapping
😊	Smile

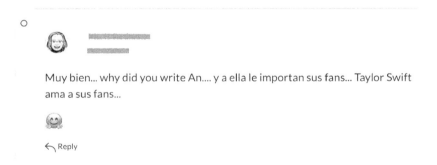

Figure 2. Sample discussion post using emojis.

incentive for completing the pretest (5 points) and posttest (5 points). Researchers could not identify answers submitted by individual students, but students' pretest and posttest responses could be matched for analysis.

Results

A paired t-test was conducted to examine students' perceptions of their instructor's presence following exposure to instructor emojis in online discussion compared to no exposure to emojis. A scale was created by summing student responses to the 14 survey items; Cronbach's alpha showed strong reliability (α = .93). There was no significant difference in students' perceptions of their online instructor when exposed to emojis (M = 55.15, SD = 10.52) compared to students who were not exposed to emojis (M = 62.58. SD, 10.33); t(23) = -.250, p = .810. These results indicate that emojis in online discussions are not sufficient to impact students' perceptions of their online instructor. Therefore, the null hypothesis is rejected: the use of emojis in online discussions did not increase students' perception of the online instructor's human presence.

CONCLUSIONS

There are several possible explanations for why the use of emojis failed to impact students' perception of instructor presence significantly: limited experience of instructor use of emojis in the context of course feedback, students' limited exposure to the emojis because they did not read the instructor's discussion feedback, and limiting the use of emojis to three online discussions. The small sample size (N = 8) may have impacted the results. The use of emojis may also be extended beyond online discussions to increase exposure. Replication of this study is warranted, with increased sample size and increased exposure to emojis. Too, replication is recommended because conveying instructor care, presence, and emotional investment in students in an online environment remains a challenge for many instructors. Using emojis as part of a robust approach to incorporating feedback with a human touch can improve student satisfaction and success.

REFERENCES

Akyol, Z., & Garrison, D. R. (2008). The development of a community of inquiry over time in an online course: Understanding the progression and integration of social, cognitive, and teaching presence. *Journal of Asynchronous Learning Networks, 12*(3-4), 3–22.

Alshenqeeti, H. (2016). Are emojis creating a new or old visual language for new generations? A socio-semiotic study. *Advances in Language and Literary Studies, 7*(6), 56–69. https://doi.org/10.7575/aiaic.alls.v.7n.6p.56

Anderson, J. F. (1979). Teacher immediacy as a predictor of teaching effectiveness. In D. Nimmo (Ed.), *Communication yearbook 3* (pp. 543–559). Transaction Books.

Appana, S. (2008). A review of benefits and limitations of online learning in the content of the student, the instructor, and the tenured faculty. *International Journal on E-Learning, 7*(1), 5–22. https://www.learntechlib.org/primary/p/22909/

Aslanian, C. B., & Clinefelter, D. L. (2013). *Online college students 2013: Comprehensive data on demands and preferences*. The Learning House.

Azuma, J. (2012). Graphic emoticons as a future universal symbolic language. *Approaches to Translation Studies, 36*, 61–84.

Bart, M. (2016, February 6). How to add the human element to online learning. *Faculty Focus.* https://www.facultyfocus.com/articles/online-education/how-to-add-the-human-element-to-online-learning/

Bartneck, C., Kulić, D., Croft, E., Zoghbi, S. (2009). Measurement instruments for the anthropomorphism, animacy, likeability, perceived intelligence, and perceived safety of robots. *International Journal of Social Robotics, 1*(1), 71–81. https://doi.org/10.1007/s12369-008-001-3

Bayne, S. (2005). Deceit, desire and control: The identities of learners and teachers in cyberspace. In R. Land & S. Bayne (Eds.), *Education in cyberspace* (pp. 26–41). Routledge.

Bollden, K. (2016). Teachers' embodied presence in online teaching practices. *Studies in Continuing Education, 38*(1), 1–15. https://doi.org/10.1080/0158037X.2014.988701

Campbell, D. T., & Stanley, J. C. (1963). *Experimental and quasi-experimental designs for research*. Houghton Mifflin.

Casey, R. L., & Kroth, M. (2013). Learning to develop a presence online: Experienced faculty perspectives. *Journal of Adult Education, 42*(2), 104–110.

Caspi, A., & Blau, I. (2008). Social presence in online discussion groups: Testing three conceptions and their relations to perceived learning. *Social Psychology of Education, 11,* 232–346. https://doi.org/10.1007/s11218-008-9054-2

Clark-Gordon, C. V., Bowman, N. D., Watts, E. R., Banks, J., & Knight, J. M. (2018). As good as your word: Face-threat mitigation and the use of instructor nonverbal cues on students' perceptions of digital feedback. *Communication Education, 67*(2), 206–225. https://doi.org/1080/03634523.2018.1428759

Clark, R. (1994). The digital persona and its application to data surveillance. *The Information Society, 10*(2), 77–92. https://doi.org/10.1080/01972243.1994.9960160

Cole, A. W., Anderson, C., Bunton, T., Cherney, M. R., Disher, V. C., Draeger, R., Featherston, M., Motel, L., Nicolini, K. M., Peck, B., & Allen, M. (2017). Student predisposition to instructor feedback and perceptions of teaching presence predicts motivation toward online courses. *Online Learning, 21*(4), 245–262. https://doi.org/10.24059/olj.v21i4.966

Conceição, S. C. O. (2006). Faculty lived experiences in the online environment. *Adult Education Quarterly, 57*(1), 26–45. https://doi.org/10.1177/1059601106292247

Cunningham, J. M. (2015). Mechanizing people and pedagogy: Establishing social presence in the online classroom. *Online Learning, 19*(3), 34–47. Retrieved from ERIC database (EJ1067482).

Danesi, M. (2016). *The semiotics of emoji: The rise of visual language in the age of the internet.* Bloomsbury.

Daymont, T., Blau, G., & Campbell, D. (2011). Deciding between traditional and online formats: Exploring the role of learning advantages, flexibility, and compensatory adaptation. *Journal of Behavioral and Applied Management, 12*(2), 156–175.

de Kerckhove, D., & de Almeida, C. M. (2013). What is a digital persona? *Technoetic Arts: A Journal of Speculative Research, 11*(3), 277–297. https://doi.org/10.1386/tear.11.3.277_1

Delaney, J., Johnson, A. N., Johnson, T. D., & Treslan, D. L. (2010). Students' perceptions of effecting teaching in higher education. Distance Education and Learning Technologies.

Diebel, P. L., & Grow, L. R. (2009). A comparative study of traditional instruction and distance education formats: Student characteristics and preferences. *NACTA Journal, 53*(2), 8–14.

Doiron, J. A. G. (2018). Emojis: Visual communication in higher education. *PUPIL: International Journal of Teaching, Education and Learning, 2*(2), 1–11. https://doi.org/10.20319/pijtel.2018.22.0111

Emoji Research Team. (2016). *2016 emoji report.* https://www.emogi.com/insights/view/report/1145/2016-emoji-report

Full emoji list, v11.0. (2018). https://unicode.org/emoji/charts/full-emoji-list.html

Garrison, D. T., Anderson, T., & Archer, W. (2000). Critical inquiry in text-based environment: Computer conferencing in higher education. *Internet and Higher Education, 2*(2-3), 87–105.

Garrison, D. T., Anderson, T., & Archer, W. (2003). A theory of critical inquiry in online distance education. In M. G. Moore & W. G. Anderson (Eds.), *Handbook of distance education* (pp. 113–128). Erlbaum.

Garrison, D. T., Cleveland-Innes, M., & Fung, T. S. (2010). Exploring casual relationships among teaching, cognitive and social presence: Student perceptions of the community of inquiry framework. *Internet and Higher Education, 13*(1), 31–36.

Gulson, T. T. (2016). You tell me in emojis. In T. Ogata & T. Akimoto (Eds.), *Computational and cognitive approaches to narratology.* IGI Global. https://doi.org/10.4018/978-1-5225-0432-0.ch014

Gunawardena, C. N., & Zittle, F. J. (1997). Social presence as a predictor of satisfaction within a computer-mediated conferencing environment. *The American Journal of Distance Education, 11*(3), 8–12.

Heap, T. (2017, June 5). *5 benefits of studying online (vs. face-to-face classroom).* Illinois Online. http://online.illinois.edu/articles/online-learning/item/2017/06/05/5-benefits-of-studying-online-(vs.-face-to-face-classroom)

Kaye, L. K., Wall, H. J., & Malone, S. A. (2016). Turn that frown upside-down: A contextual account of emoticon usage on different virtual platforms. *Computers in Human Behavior, 60*(C), 463-467. https://doi.org/10.1016/j.chb.2016.02.088

Kear, K., Chetwynd, F., & Jefferis, H. (2014). Social presence in online communities: The role of personal profiles. *Research in Learning Technology, 22,* Article 1970.

Kerssen-Griep, J., & Witt, P. L. (2012). Instructional feedback II: How do instructor immediacy cues and facework tactics interact to predict student motivation and fairness perceptions. *Communication Studies, 63*(4), 498–517. https://doi.org/10.1080/10510974.2011.632660

Kumar, S., Daweson, K., Black, E. W., Cavanaugh, C., & Sessums, C. D. (2011). Applying the community of inquiry framework to an online professional practice doctoral program. *International Review of Research in Open and Distance Learning, 12*(6). http://www.irrodl.org/index.php/irrodl/article/view/978/1961

Lee, S. J., & Huang, K. (2018). Online interactions and social presence in online learning. (2018). *Journal of Interactive Learning Research, 29*(1), 113–128.

Lehman, R. M., & Conceição, S. C. O. (2010). *Creating a sense of presence in online teaching: How to "be there" for distance learners.* Jossey-Bass.

Leong, P. (2011). Role of social presence and cognitive absorption in online learning environments. *Distance Education, 32*(1), 5–28.

Mathieson, K., & Leafman, J. S. (2014). Comparison of student and instructor perceptions of social presence. *Journal of Educators Online, 11*(2). ERIC database. (EJ1033262)

McIntyre, E. S. (2016). *From cave paintings to Shakespeare and back again: What are emoji and should I be afraid?* [Unpublished thesis]. Texas State University.

McQuiggan, C. A. (2012). Faculty development for online teaching as a catalyst for change. *Journal of Asynchronous Learning Networks, 16*(2), 27–61. ERIC database. (EJ971044)

Miller, H., Thebault-Spieker, J., Chang, S., Johnson, I., Terveen, L., & Hecht, B. (2016). "Blissfully happy" or "ready to fight": Varying interpretations of emoji. In *Proceedings of the 10th International Conference on Web and Social Media* (pp. 259–268). AAAI Press.

Moschini, I. (2016). The "face with tears of joy" emoji: A socio-semiotic and multimodal insight into a Japan-America mash-up. *HERMES–Journal of Language and Communication Business, 55,* 11–25.

Muilenburg, L. Y., & Berge, Z. L. (2005). Student barriers to online learning: A factor analytic study. *Distance Education, 26*(1), 29–48.

Riordan, M. A. (2017). Emojis as tools for emotion work: Communicating affect in text messages. *Journal of Language and Social Psychology, 36*(5), 549–567. https://doi.org/10.1177/0261927X17704238

Rodriquez, F. G., & Nash, S. S. (2004). Technology and the adult degree program: The human element. *New Directions for Adult and Continuing Education, 103,* 73–79.

Sarsar, F. (2017). Student and instructor responses to emotional motivational feedback messages in an online instructional environment. *The Turkish Online Journal of Educational Technology, 16*(1), 115–127.

Short, J. E., Williams, E., & Christie, B. (1976). *The social psychology of telecommunications.* Wiley.

Skiba, D. J. (2016). Face with tears of joy is a word of the year: Are emoji a sign of things to come in health care? *Nursing Education Perspectives, 37*(1), 56–57.

Sung, E., & Mayer, R. E. (2012). Five facets of social presence in online distance education. *Computers in Human Behavior, 28,* 1738–1747.

Tauch, C., & Kanjo, E. (2016). The roles of emojis in mobile phone applications. In *Proceedings of the 2016 ACM International Joint Conference on Pervasive and Ubiquitous Computing: Adjunct* (pp. 1560–1565).

Tichavsky, L. P., Hunt, A. N., Driscoll, A., & Jocha, K. (2015). "It's just nice having a real teacher": Student perceptions of online versus face-to-face instruction. *International Journal for the Scholarship of Teaching and Learning, 9*(2), 1–8. https://doi.org/10.20429/ijsotl.2015.090202

University of Central Florida. (2018). *University of Central Florida 2018–2018 undergraduate catalog.* http://catalog.ucf.edu/index.php?catoid=3

Wall, H. J., Kaye, L. K., & Malone, S. A. (2016). An exploration of psychological factors on emoticon usage and implications for judgment accuracy. *Computers in Human Behavior, 62,* 70–78. https://doi.org/10.1016/j.chb.2016.03.040

Walther, J. (1994). Interpersonal effects in computer-mediated interaction. *Communication Research, 12*(4), 460–487.

Watson, W. R., & Watson, S. L. (2007). An argument for clarity: What are learning management systems, what are they not, and what should they become? *TechTrends, 51*(2), 28–34.

Wei, C., Chen, N., & Kinshuk. (2012). A model for social presence in online classrooms. *Educational Technology Research and Development, 60*(3), 529–545. ERIC database. (EJ965847)

Yuasa, M., Saito, K., & Mukawa, N. (2011). Brain activity when reading sentences and emoticons: An fMRI study of verbal and non-verbal communication. *Electronics and Communications in Japan, 94*(5), 17–24. https://doi.org/10.2002/ecj.10311

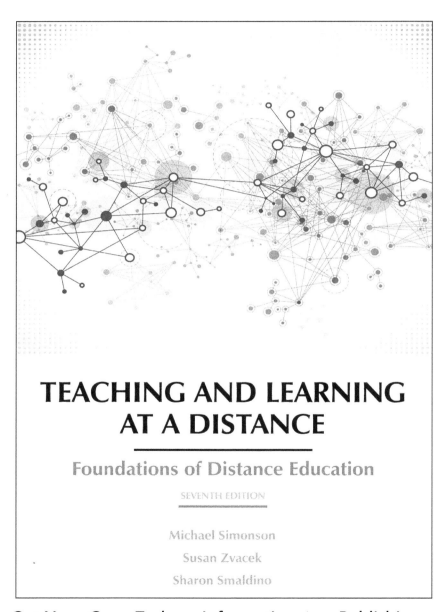

Get Your Copy Today—Information Age Publishing

Evaluation and Investigation of Prescience Teachers' Perceptions Toward Distance Education

Nesrin Ürün Arici and Emre Yildiz

This research aimed to evaluate the perceptions of prescience teachers about distance education at a state university in Turkey during the COVID-19 pandemic. The participants of the research, selected with the criterion sampling technique, consisted of 50 prescience teachers studying at a state university in the 2020–2021 academic year. As the data collection tool in the research, Perception of the Distance Education Students About Distance Education scale and the semistructured interview created by the researchers were used. Content analysis and descriptive statistics were used in the analysis. According to the research results, half of the preservice teachers think face-to-face education might be better than distance lessons because face-to-face education is more effective and efficient than distance education. Preservice teachers did not prefer distance education because

Nesrin Ürün Arici,
PhD Student, Department of Science Education, Kazim Karabekir Education Faculty, Ataturk University, Erzurum, Turkey, 0000-0003-3394-4860.
Email: nurunarici@gmail.com

Emre Yildiz,
Dr., Associate Professor, Department of Science Education, Kazım Karabekir Education Faculty, Atatürk University, Erzurum, Turkey, 0000-0001-6396-9183.
Email: emre.yildiz@atauni.edu.tr

of application inadequacy, technological inadequacy, lack of efficiency, and lack of opportunities. The other halves of preservice science teachers thought that lessons were better remotely. They preferred distance education in terms of safety and where they can benefit from research opportunities and technological opportunities. Also, it was determined that preservice teachers thought distance education is effective, interactive, providing active learning, drawing attention, and benefiting from technological applications.

Keywords: distance education, perception, prescience teachers

INTRODUCTION

The worldwide COVID-19 pandemic has profoundly changed almost all aspects of life, including education (Aliyyah et al., 2020). The recent transition from face-to-face to distance education due to the pandemic is a change in education. These changes can affect the trainer and the person being trained and their circumstances. In addition, distance education is a developing situation at the intersection of human-computer interaction, instructional technology, and cognitive science. So, moving to teach online can provide the flexibility of teaching and learning anywhere, anytime. However, this transition to distance education has been faster and more surprising than expected (Hodges et al., 2020). Distance education has become known for its separation from the conditions in which teaching and learning occur naturally (Larreamendy-Joerns & Leinhardt, 2006). Technology has played and continues to play an important role in developing and expanding distance education. Accordingly, many universities have reported an increase in remotely operated tools.

In the last decade, with this increase, numerous efforts have been made to integrate Internet technologies into the teaching and learning process in higher education (Kim & Bonk, 2006). The emergence of distance education affects the faculty, those who teach remotely, and those experimenting with web-based elements blended with traditional classrooms (Mayadas et al., 2009). Moreover, a review of the literature considers student achievement and satisfaction as two ways of assessing the quality of distance education. Various research studies on student satisfaction in online courses or programs have reported that students are both satisfied and dissatisfied (Kim & Bonk, 2006). Especially when these studies are examined, besides the studies focusing on academic achievement, some researchers point out that distance education can be at least as effective as current classroom education (Kim & Bonk, 2006). Therefore, distance education's progress and learning effectiveness largely depend on students' high-level active learning at a distance.

Consequently, it may be appropriate for faculty to use various methods to reinforce students' distance active learning (Bao, 2020). As the literature is examined, it is possible to come across studies on distance education. These studies evaluate feedback on web-based education, distance learning systems, and their effects on student achievement. In addition, studies have also examined the extent to which interaction and other predictors contribute to student satisfaction in distance learning environments.

Moreover, it was investigated how distance learning self-efficacy, learner-content interaction, learner-instructor interaction, and learner-learner interaction can predict student satisfaction and perceived learning (Alqurashi, 2019; Keskin & Özer, 2020; Kuo et al., 2013; Lai et al., 2019). The study results show that, while the effectiveness of distance education is accepted by most of the students, it has been revealed that distance education is not as effective as face-to-face education. It can be said that students' success can be directly proportional to their satisfaction, perception, the methods used by the instructors, the conditions they were facing, and the types of interaction. In the light of the literature reviewed, it may be important to conduct the lessons in the form of distance education during the pandemic process to evaluate the advantages, disadvantages, and reflections of the distance education structured according to the feedback of the students and to structure the distance education following the students' situations in this direction. Since while student satisfaction and positive perceptions are used as key elements in evaluating the courses they take, it is also accepted as an indicator of learning. Since student satisfaction and positive perceptions are critical elements in evaluating their courses, it is also accepted as an indicator of learning. However, for this process to be carried out correctly, higher education does not know the details of the process, how students access and configure information, the programs they can use remotely, the situations they live in, the progress or difficulties in their development. In addition, in faculties of higher education, training 21st-century teachers who are well equipped in their fields and pedagogical education is essential for the future of society. Also, it was thought that the 21st century need for teachers could be supplied by working with preservice teachers. At the end of this research, faculty will be able to communicate well with preservice teachers and guide them in their teaching-learning process. In addition, as a result of this study, it can shed light on and improve the distance education preparations and the situations that may be encountered in the future courses of the universities.

In this way, interruptions or problems students face in education can be minimized. Based on this situation, the study aims to determine the most effective communication for preservice science teachers who continue their education remotely at a state university in Turkey during the COVID-19 pandemic, to determine the internet-based platforms they use and the duration of use, to evaluate the distance education methods and students' perceptions about distance education. In line with this purpose, "What are the perceptions of preservice science teachers toward conducting distance education courses in recent years?" the answer to the question has been determined.

Method

Phenomenological design, one of the qualitative research types, was used in this research. The phenomenological method studies the experiences of individuals in-depth and focuses on the meaning of these idioms for individuals (Creswell, 1998). In this study, the most appropriate method is the phenomenological method, since it is aimed to determine in detail the perceptions of preservice teachers about distance education applied during the pandemic period.

Participants

This research studied 50 preservice science teachers at a state university in the 2020–2021 academic year. The criterion sampling method selected preservice teachers for the participant group. Criterion sampling is the study of situations that meet a set of predetermined criteria (Yıldırım & Şimşek, 2016). The research determined class attendance as a criterion, and 52 preservice teachers, 13 from each grade level, attended the classes at the maximum level for two semesters. Volunteering was wanted in the selected preservice teachers, and two preservice teachers who did not want to participate in the research were not included. In the second stage of the research, 10 preservice teachers were conducted with the maximum sampling method. Maximum diversity sampling enables the problem situation to be examined on a broader framework by revealing the homogeneous and separate aspects between different situations in line with the determined purpose (Yıldırım & Şimşek, 2016). At this stage, preservice teachers with different characteristics were selected, taking into account gender, school average scores, grade level, and their view toward online education.

DATA COLLECTION TOOLS

The Opinion Scale for Distance Education used in the research was developed by Yıldırım et al. (2014). The scale was based on studies that included views on distance education. In addition, the developed 42-item scale was applied to the students online. In the pilot applications, 1,040 students in the distance education program of Atatürk University were studied. The scale was finalized by evaluating the data with principal component analysis. The final version of the scale's research results consisted of 18 items and included four factors (personal relevance, effectiveness, instructiveness, and appropriateness). The Cronbach alpha coefficient of the internal consistency analysis of the whole scale was calculated as 0.86. Internal consistency coefficients were 0.86 for the "personal suitability" subdimension; 0.82 for "effectiveness"; It was measured as 0.81 for "Instructiveness" and 0.80 for "familiarity." For this study, exploratory and confirmatory factor analyzes were carried out in the validity studies of the scale. It was determined that the factor distributions were provided, and the goodness of fit indices was at a good level. For this study, the scale's Cronbach alpha internal consistency coefficient was calculated as 0.84. The internal consistency coefficients were 0.79 for the personal suitability subdimension, 0.83 for the effectiveness subdimension, 0.83 for the instructiveness subdimension, and 0.81 for the familiarity subdimension.

A semistructured opinion form was prepared to determine preservice teachers' opinions about applied distance education. This form included questions about the way of education, positive and limited aspects of distance education, programs used in distance education, materials, measurement-evaluation methods, and problems encountered. The prepared interview questions were presented to two field experts who took part in distance education and worked on this topic, and the experts stated that the questions could be used as they are. The pilot application of the form was made by selecting three preservice teachers participating in the research. As a result of the pilot application, it was determined that the questions in the opinion form were understandable, and the form served its purpose. The interview form was presented to the preservice teachers online. Before analyzing the data obtained from the interview form, it was examined how many minutes the preservice teachers allocated to each question in the form. It was determined that the time allocated to the questions was sufficient.

DATA COLLECTION PROCESS

This study aimed to investigate the perceptions of preservice science teachers. Due to the COVID-19 pandemic, the Opinion Scale for Distance Education was first applied to evaluate preservice science teachers' views about distance education within the scope of the distance teaching of the courses. Semistructured interviews were also conducted with ten preservice teachers from the sample to which the scale was applied. The interviews aimed to determine the most effective communication way of preservice teachers, the internet-based platforms they use and the duration of use, the evaluation of distance education methods, and students' perceptions about distance education.

DATA ANALYSIS

In this research, SPSS 22 program was used to analyze descriptive statistics obtained from the opinion scale for distance education. The content analysis method was used to analyze the data obtained from the semistructured interview form. First, structural codes were created by reading the answers given by the preservice teachers repeatedly. The codes are given to the relevant parts. Codes are combined under similar categories. The codes are presented under the related themes. Examples of preservice teachers' responses are given. Analyzes were carried out by two researchers independent of each other. The data were analyzed independently by two researchers. The percentage of agreement between the analyzes of the two researchers was calculated with the Miles Huberman formula. The percentage of agreement for the researcher's notes was 79%, and the percentage of agreement for the preservice teachers' opinions was 76%. It can be said that reliability is achieved if the compliance percentages are 70% or more (Miles & Huberman, 1994).

RESULTS AND DISCUSSION

The results of the descriptive statistics analysis, which were conducted to determine the level of preservice teachers' views on distance education, are given in Table 1.

According to the results of the analysis given in Table 1, views of the preservice teachers toward distance education are below the average in the subdimensions of personal suitability and aptitude, above the average in the subdimension of effectiveness in the subdimension of teaching and generally at an average level.

The opinions of the preservice teachers about the form of education and the analysis results of the reasons for their preference are given in Figure 1.

Figure 1 shows the preservice teachers reported mainly positive opinions about AR with integrated modeling, and their answers were grouped under four themes. According to the results of the analysis given in Figure 1, most preservice teachers prefer face-to-face education. They think that face-to-face education is effective, understandable, and permanent. In addition, preservice teachers do not prefer online education due to the inadequacy of the application, technological inadequacy, lack of efficiency, and lack of opportunities. However, preservice teachers who prefer online education think that online education is comfortable, healthy, abundant resources, and easy to access. The analysis results of prospective teachers' views on effective and meaningful learning in online education are given in Figure 2.

According to the analysis results given in Figure 2, preservice teachers mostly think that meaningful and effective learning occurs at a moderate level in online education. The analysis results of the preservice teachers' views on the programs they prefer to use in online education,

Table 1. Descriptive Statistics Results
of Preservice Teachers' Opinions on Distance Education

Subdimensions	N	Min	Max	Mean	Median	Df
Personal suitability	50	9,00	22,00	16,90	17,00	2,77
Effectiveness	50	15,00	24,00	20,44	21,00	2,51
Instructiveness	50	7,00	16,00	12,12	12,00	2,19
Familiarity	50	3,00	9,00	4,28	3,00	1,69
Total	50	44,00	66,00	55,10	55,00	4,16

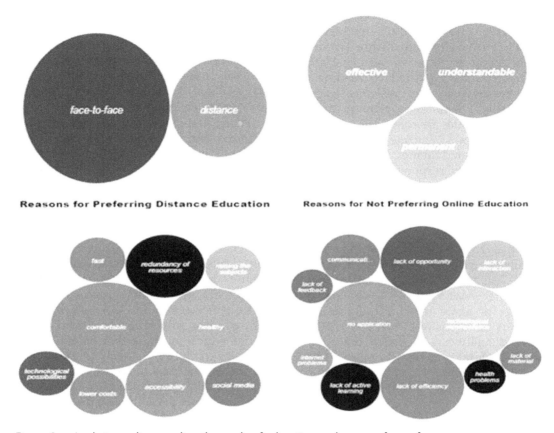

Figure 1. Analysis results regarding the mode of education and reasons for preference.

measurement-evaluation, and methods of putting knowledge into practice are given in Figure 3.

As can be seen from the analysis results given in Figure 3, preservice teachers mostly use Zoom, online education provided by the university infrastructure, and Google document applications. It is seen that some of the preservice teachers do not prefer to use any program in online education. In addition, it was determined that the most frequently encountered assessment-evaluation applications by preservice teachers are question-answer, subject test, and online exams using mixed types of questions. They prefer applications such as doing homework, adapting to sample situations, and actively participating in the lesson to put the knowledge into practice.

The results of the analysis of the preservice teachers' opinions about the effectiveness of online education are given in Figure 4.

According to the results of the analysis given in Figure 4, it was determined that preservice teachers think that for online education to be effective, the education should be applied and interactive, active learning should be provided, attention should be drawn, technological applica-

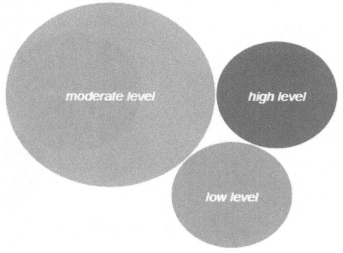

Figure 2. Opinions on effective and meaningful learning in online education.

tions should be utilized, and a plan should be made.

Examples of preservice teachers' answers are presented below:

> It should be done face to face because effective learning does not take place with distance education. In addition, some students are depressed about the lack of materials in applied courses and as a result of laboratory education. From our point of view, we will be science teachers, so our laboratory culture must be very good, but this is not possible with distance education. (Preservice Teacher 5)

> The platforms I use most often in distance education are Xuni and Zoom. Zoom is more functional in terms of coursework. However, Xuni is more advantageous in terms of recording and replayability of the lesson. (Preservice Teacher 10)

> I think there is less interaction in class. For the teacher-student relationship. … There is not the slightest activity that we will do. (Preservice Teacher 4)

> The cost of distance education is lower than face-to-face education; it provides opportunities for students who cannot access face-to-face education and allows us to listen to the course recording again. (Preservice Teacher 3)

CONCLUSION

As a result of this research, the following has been found:

Half of the preservice teachers prefer face-to-face education, and the other half prefer distance education. Preservice teachers who prefer face-to-face education generally stated that face-to-face education is more effective and efficient than distance education. This result is similar to Pepeler et al. (2018) studies. As a result of the study, they determined that the students thought distance education was ineffective in improving their knowledge.

Preservice teachers do not prefer distance education due to application, technological inadequacy, lack of efficiency, and lack of opportunities. This result is similar to Akca's (2006) study, based on student impressions, which are communication barriers including technical barriers, psy-

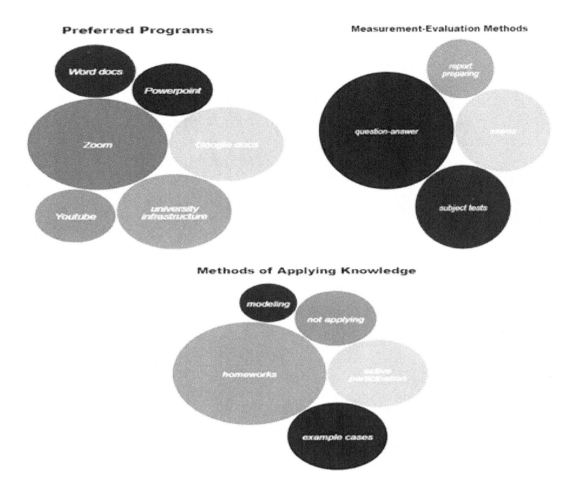

Figure 3. Preferred programs of preservice teachers in online education, assessment-evaluation, and knowledge application methods.

chological barriers, personal barriers, distance barriers, interruption barriers, and time pressure barriers. Also similarly, Karakus et al. (2020) concluded that the most common technical setbacks are internet/connection problems and unsupported device/hardware deficiency. In addition, it is found that distance education compared to face-to-face education has more disadvantages such as infrastructure problems, lack of active learning, and communication problems.

Preservice teachers prefer distance education types that are safer and where they can benefit from research opportunities and technological opportunities. In addition, they expressed opinions that distance education is comfortable, healthy, resources are abundant, and access is easy. This result is similar to the studies of Kırali and Bülent (2016) and Paydar and Doğan (2019). They stated that most preservice teachers had a positive opinion about distance learning, the course was useful, and they were willing to take the course. Preservice teachers mostly think that meaningful and effective learning in distance education occurs at a moderate level. In other words, distance education is effective. However, preservice teachers are not inclined to do this.

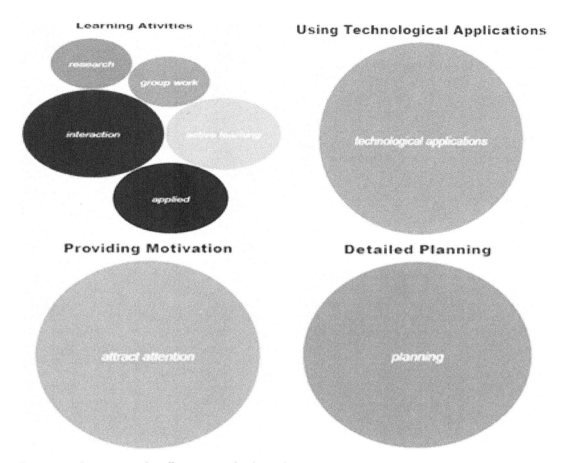

Figure 4. Opinions on the effectiveness of online education.

While some of the preservice teachers generally prefer applications such as Zoom, Google Classroom, Google Docs, PowerPoint, and Word in distance education, it is determined that some of them do not prefer to use any program in distance education. In this case, it can be said that Web 2.0 tools are not used at all, and that preservice teachers are insufficient in digital learning. In addition, it was stated that the assessment-evaluation applications most frequently encountered by preservice teachers were question-answer, subject tests, and online exams using mixed-type questions. Meanwhile, it was determined that they preferred applications such as doing homework, adapting to sample situations, and actively participating in the lesson to put the knowledge into practice. The preservice teachers' opinions were determined that for distance education to be effective, education should be applied and interactive, active learning should be provided, attention should be drawn, technological applications should be utilized, and a plan should be made. In addition, it has been stated that distance education is advantageous compared to face-to-face education in terms of low cost, easily accessible, safe, technological opportunities and resources.

It has been determined that preservice teachers' views about distance education are average. In summary, it has been concluded that distance education has advantages and disadvantages compared to face-to-face education. Therefore, both education situations do not have superiority over each other. Finally, it can be suggested that relevant experts strengthen the infrastructure of the distance education system, use more technology-based platforms such as Web 2.0 tools, and provide infrastructure support to trainers and students.

REFERENCES

Akca, Ö. (2006). *Demands of the SAU distance education students according to communication barriers* [Master thesis]. Sakarya University. Sakarya.

Aliyyah, R. R., Rachmadtullah, R., Samsudin, A., Syaodih, E., Nurtanto, M., & Tambunan, A. R. S. (2020). The perceptions of primary school teachers of online learning during the COVID-19 pandemic period: A case study in Indonesia. *Journal of Ethnic and Cultural Studies, 7*(2), 90–109.

Alqurashi, E. (2019). Predicting student satisfaction and perceived learning within online learning environments. *Distance Education, 40*(1), 133–148.

Bao, W. (2020). COVID-19 and online teaching in higher education: A case study of Peking University. *Human Behavior and Emerging Technologies, 2*(2), 113–115.

Creswell, J. W. (1998). *Qualitative inquiry and research design: Choosing among five traditions.* SAGE.

Hodges, C., Moore, S., Lockee, B., Trust, T., & Bond, A. (2020). The difference between emergency remote teaching and online learning. *Educause Review, 27*, 1–12.

Karakuş, N., Ucuzsatar, N., Karacaoğlu, M. Ö., Esendemir, N., & Bayraktar, D. (2020). Turkish teacher candidates' views on distance education. *RumeliDE Journal of Language and Literature Studies, 19*, 220–241.

Keskin, M., & Özer, D., (2020). Evaluation of students' feedbacks on web-based distance education in the COVID-19 process. *Journal of Izmir Katip Celebi University Faculty of Health Sciences, 5*(2), 59–67.

Kim, K. J., & Bonk, C. J. (2006). The future of online teaching and learning in higher education. *Educause Quarterly, 29*(4), 22–30.

Kırali, F. N., & Bülent, A. L. C. I. (2016). University student opinions regarding the perception of distance education. *Journal of Istanbul Aydın University, 8*(30), 55–83.

Kuo, Y. C., Walker, A. E., Belland, B. R., & Schroder, K. E. (2013). A predictive study of student satisfaction in online education programs. *International Review of Research in Open and Distributed Learning, 14*(1), 16–39.

Lai, C. H., Lin, H. W., Lin, R. M., & Tho, P. D. (2019). Effect of peer interaction among online learning community on learning engagement and achievement. *International Journal of Distance Education Technologies (IJDET), 17*(1), 66–77.

Larreamendy-Joerns, J., & Leinhardt, G. (2006). Going the distance with online education. *Review of Educational Research, 76*(4), 567–605.

Mayadas, A. F., Bourne, J., & Bacsich, P. (2009). Online education today. *Science, 323*(5910), 85–89.

Miles, M. B., & Huberman, A. M. (1994). *Qualitative data analysis: An expanded sourcebook* (2nd ed.). SAGE.

Paydar, S., & Doğan, A. (2019). Teacher candidates' views on open and distance learning environments. *Education & Technology, 1*(2), 154–162.

Pepeler, E., Özbek, R., & Adanır, Y. (2018). Students' views on English lesson taught through distance education: Mus Alparslan University sample. *Anemon Journal of Social Sciences of Mus Alparslan University, 6*(3), 421–429.

Yıldırım, A., & Şimşek, H. (2016). *Qualitative research methods in the social sciences* (9th ed.). Seçkin Press.

Yıldırım, S., Yıldırım, G., Çelik, E., & Karaman, S. (2014). Perception of distance education students about distance education: A scale development study. *Journal of Research in Education and Teaching, 3*(3), 365–370.

Ends and Means

Preparing for and Cultivating Instructional Continuity in Online Courses

Natalie B. Milman

A common challenge that most instructors face at some point while teaching in higher education is how to prepare for and cultivate instructional continuity. According to Milman and Watkins (2021), "Instructional continuity, sometimes referred to as academic continuity or continuity of teaching and learning, is the capacity to maintain course schedules when plans are disrupted, typically by unanticipated events beyond anyone's control" (Milman & Watkins, 2021, para. 1). Examples of unanticipated events are natural (e.g., snowstorm) or human-made (e.g., mass shooting) disasters. In some cases, there is ample notice to prepare such as might be the case with a hurricane whose trajectory is forecast accurately; however, with others, there is no time to get things in order as is the case with an earthquake or terrorist attack. Also, Mitroff et al. (2006) noted that there are also "ticking time bombs" (p. 6), such as unethical or criminal behavior, that pose unique challenges and can explode and spread with unanticipated consequences. Clearly, we are living during very uncertain times—what can instructors do to be ready to address any disruptions that might occur? Below are some suggestions to consider when preparing for instructional continuity for teaching online.

Natalie B. Milman,
Professor of Educational Technology,
George Washington University, Graduate
School of Education & Human Development,
2134 G ST, NW, Washington DC 20052.
Telephone: (202) 994-1884.
Email: nmilman@gwu.edu

PROACTIVELY CONTACT STUDENTS

If bad weather is forecast where some (or all) students reside, it is good practice to contact these students early to (1) share resources to support their well-being, (2) explain how to contact you if they experience any challenges and are unable to be actively involved in the course (e.g., they can contact the program director and then the program director will contact all of their instructors so there's just one communication shared and not multiple during stressful times).

DEVELOP BACK-UP PLANS

Create plans if something interferes with your asynchronous or synchronous online courses. For example, if presenting lecture content synchronously, be sure to provide all students information about what to do if they have trouble viewing the presentation (often web conferencing tools will work better with the video camera off and the sounds on but muted).

PRACTICE RUN

The old saying that "practice makes perfect" is very meaningful here. The success of any tool, let alone a whole remote learning day where learning depends on the tools used and the knowledge of those using it, will be more successful if everyone has had the opportunity to practice using the tools and technologies. Additionally, a practice run will provide students the opportunity to address any issues they might encounter.

PROVIDE PDFS OF LECTURE MATERIALS IN ADVANCE

If/when students might (or do) experience disruption, it helps if instructors share course materials in PDF format with students. Using PDFs of course materials should allow students to print and then later read the materials anywhere/anytime without needing to have internet or even electricity.

COLLECT STUDENTS' ALTERNATE CONTACT INFO

At the beginning of the semester, it is important to ask students to share unique information about them, as well as their preferred phone number and alternate email address to contact them. Often the information in the university registrar system and the LMS is inaccurate. Having up-to-date contact information is very important, as well as information about their preferred contact methods (e.g., many students do not read email but do respond to text messages). Also, the unique information collected might be very valuable in understanding how to best support and teach students.

USE TECHNOLOGY TO CONTACT STUDENTS

There are many different ways to contact one's students. Determine the best methods and technologies (e.g., instant messaging, phone call) for reaching them while also protecting their privacy. There are a variety of apps, such as GroupMe (https://groupme.com/en-US/) or Signal (https://signal.org/en/), that allow group members to message one another without sharing their personal phone numbers.

COMMUNICATE EXPECTATIONS

In any course, communicating expectations is extremely important. This can be done in formal (e.g., share a policy of the frequency and when you will respond to student email and/or requests to meet or conference) and informal ways (such as via a course announcement). Also, be sure to have a backup plan if you lose power or internet.

FLEXIBLE LATE ASSIGNMENT POLICY

Having a flexible assignment policy for late work due to unexpected disruptions to the course LMS will help students not only manage disruption, but also support their success. Often, disruption is out of the student's hands.

DEVELOP AND SCHEDULE LECTURES TO START/LAUNCH

Most learning management systems such as Blackboard, Canvas, or Moodle, allow instructors to schedule when a lecture will launch. For online courses, it is good practice to populate all or as much of the course content as possible in one's courses and then to schedule when the content will become available to students. By setting up content to open up on a schedule, not only do students know what to expect but it also provides instructors with structure and a mechanism for launching content automatically—even if they are unable to do so.

BECOME FAMILIAR WITH INSTITUTIONAL POLICIES AND PRACTICES

Every institution has unique institutional policies and practices. It is important for all instructors to learn about the various institutional policies and practices associated with instructional continuity. Additionally, it is important for institutions of higher education to teach all instructors, including adjuncts, about the importance and need for instructional continuity planning.

PROVIDE CLEAR INSTRUCTIONS

Clear, succinct, and specific instructions go a long way for promoting student success. We recommend that you include clear instructions about how to access and engage with materials, your peers, and instructor.

Overall, this is just a start of some things instructors can do in their online courses to foster instructional continuity. It is likely some students will require more hand-holding and support than others. This is always the case—and attribution should not go toad

REFERENCES

Milman, N. B., & Watkins, R. (2021). Designing with instructional continuity in mind. In J. E. Stefaniak, S. Conklin, B. Oyarzun, & R. Reese (Eds.). *A practitioner's guide to instructional design in higher education*. EdTechBooks. https://edtechbooks.org/id_highered/designing_with_instr

Mitroff, I. I., Diamond, M. A., & Alpaslan, C. M. (2006). How prepared are America's colleges and universities for major crisis: Assessing the state of crisis management. *Change, 38*(1), 61–67.

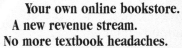

Try This

Labor-Based Grading
Perfect for Distance Learning!

Errol Craig Sull

Labor-based grading: for many instructors in the world of distance learning this is a new concept, yet it is one that is rapidly growing in acceptance and popularity. First introduced in 1993 by English professor Peter Elbow, the premise of labor-based grading is that instructors weigh assignments based on how much labor—how much "effort"—students put into their work, rather than assigning grades based on a points-based rubric or work quality.

This column is divided into two sections: (1) specifics relating to the student; (2) specifics relating to the instructor: together, this information will give you solid preparation for teaching a labor-based grading course:

SPECIFICS RELATING TO THE STUDENT

LABOR-BASED GRADING IS IDEAL FOR THE DISTANCE LEARNING CLASS

In online learning everything is available for a student to view 24/7, and this includes reminders of a student's grades, the requirements to earn full points for an assignment, and ongoing reminders from the instructor (and often from classmates as well) as to what it takes to achieve a great grade on an assignment/in the course. This constant in-your-face reminder and emphasis on grading can diminish the learning process. But when grading is gone there is a healthier, this-is-all-about-learning environment. Additionally, more emphasis can be placed in the available resources in and out of class to expand and deepen student knowledge of a subject.

Errol Craig Sull,
Faculty, Composition and Writing Across the Curriculum, Purdue Global University.
Email: erroldistancelearning@gmail.com
(for column submissions)

STUDENTS ARE MORE WILLING TO TAKE CHANCES WITH "GUT FEELINGS" ABOUT INCLUDING X OR Y INTO AN ASSIGNMENT, RATHER THAN OPTING FOR THE SAFER APPROACH THEY KNOW WILL UNDOUBTEDLY PRODUCE A GOOD GRADE

They are not penalized for taking these risks since grades are no longer a part of the assignments. This helps break students out of a "conformity learning" approach – this has probably been instilled within them throughout their academic journey – and allows for more learning experimentation and creativity, keys to improving one's knowledge and critical thinking.

STUDENTS LEARN IT IS, ULTIMATELY, THE EFFORT ONE PUTS INTO CREATING A FINISHED PRODUCT THAT PRODUCES A QUALITY PRODUCT—IN SCHOOL AND OUT

When the overriding goal for a course assignment is an A grade the broadest effort may not be employed, only that which the rubric says must be done to achieve that high mark. Yet with labor-based grading it is not the end result of an assignment or a course nor prior knowledge of a subject a student holds, but rather towards the processes of learning needed to complete each part of an assignment of a course. Students should be reminded this extends far beyond the course, and especially in the professional job market.

STUDENT QUESTIONS WILL FOCUS MORE ON HOW TO LEARN RATHER THAN HOW TO GET A GOOD GRADE

Class after class after class have found instructors responding to a variety of student questions relating to "the big one"— "What do I need do to get an A on this assignment?" This no longer exists with labor-based grading; rather, student questions will now center around a different big one: "How can I learn better?"

LABOR-BASED GRADING REDUCES STRESS, ANXIETY, AND WORRY FOR STUDENTS IN THE CLASS—AND ALSO BUILDS CONFIDENCE

Both anecdotal and research feedback show many students in a grade-based course have ongoing concerns about achieving a good grade on an assignment. Added to this is the result of receiving a grade that is disappointing. The stress, anxiety, and worry this can cause have led to students giving up in class and often dropping out of a course. Yet with an emphasis solely on the learning effort a student can feel more relaxed, not having to be concerned about a grade. There is also the bonus of improving a student's confidence in the course: ongoing strong efforts result in ongoing nice results throughout the course!

STUDENTS HAVE MORE FLEXIBILITY ON WHOM TO FOLLOW TO IMPROVE LEARNING

In assignments where the grade is the ultimate quest the instructor's feedback is usually the one students care to follow, as they believe it, and it alone, will result in that A grade. But with labor-based grading it is not pleasing the teacher or following the rubric, but rather all input—instructor, peers in class, resources—that can be embraced, for all are aimed at helping one to improve the learning effort, not to achieve a grade.

LABOR-BASED GRADING CAN BE A BOON FOR STUDENTS WHERE ENGLISH IS NOT THE PRIMARY LANGUAGE

It is no secret that students who have English as a second language can sometimes do poorly in a grade-based course due to their poor grasp of English (and at times this can extend to misunderstanding of assignment directions). Yet with labor-based grading this is no longer a concern, as it is—fully—their efforts that count. And there is a bonus: as they ply their efforts improvement in their English will also come, but at a natural, rather than a forced, pace.

LABOR-BASED GRADING CONTRACTS: WHAT THEY ARE AND HOW THEY ARE USED

Many labor-based grading courses use contracts between each student and the instructor. These contracts are a set of agreements among all class members that determine how much labor (work and time) are required for any student to receive a grade. Additionally, the contracts have no focus on judgments of the quality of writing or the quality of the assignments. A school may or may not use these contracts.

SPECIFICS RELATING TO THE INSTRUCTOR

THE INSTRUCTOR CAN SPEND MORE TIME WITH QUALITY FEEDBACK EMPHASIZING THE LEARNING PROCESS RATHER THAN NEEDING TO JUDGE A STUDENT'S ASSIGNMENT AGAINST A GRADES-BASED RUBRIC

This allows for a shift from deciding if the assignment is an A or B, et cetera effort but rather more on the effort itself—a work-in-progress, and how that work-in-progress can be improved. Additionally, the instructor no longer needs to be concerned with "Oh, boy—what if my supervisor sees the low number of As for this assignment?!" The stress, anxiety, and worry for instructors are also greatly reduced through labor-based grading.

GETTING STUDENTS TO "BUY IN" TO LABOR-BASED GRADING: A GLOBAL APPROACH IS NEEDED

The students need to realize that everything in a course applies to life outside the course, and especially important is the professional careers they seek. Overall effort is what is needed for results, whether that be success in the employment field or a grade in a course. Once solid, sustained, and focused effort is applied the task will be a successful one—and the grade in a course will be a successful one. This transitions nicely to the course, for if a student knows only the grade of an assignment and points required for each part of that assignment full effort might not be applied, only that which the student believes is needed for a good grade. Ultimately, this results in less-than-full effort, and the resulting grade usually reflects this.

AN OPTION TO UNDERSTANDING LABOR-BASED GRADING AND (WHEN APPLICABLE) CONTRACTS: GROUP SHARING

Beyond receiving input on and responses to questions about labor-based grading from the instructor, it has been found that breaking students into groups and sharing ideas, concerns, and questions among themselves can also help with students feeling more comfortable about a labor-based grading course. One approach to this is to have a "secretary" for each group jot down any items that need clarification and for which there are questions, then send this list onto the instructor. Often, this has resulted in better student buy-in (they have more ownership in the course) and the instructor may find items he or she not had initially explained or detailed to the class.

More Work for Instructors: It Depends

Each instructor has a different approach to managing a class, and this is the determining factor as to whether labor-based grading takes more time and effort. If one micromanages a course the answer might be yes, but overall it should require less time as no longer do grades need be calculated/points considered. As for new instructions, if these are not already built into a course an instructor can create labor-grading templates that give instructions for each assignment and the course.

An Important Component of Labor-Based Grading: The Equality of Each Assignment Component

In points-based grading one component of an assignment might be worth more points than another, for example, in a writing course the prewriting portion might offer far fewer points that the full essay. Yet because labor-based grading focuses on effort expended each component of an assignment would be equal, as each is graded based on effort. Additionally, components of an assignment that previously were not counted by the instructor may now be added to the "effort" category.

Suggestions to Help Students Succeed in a Labor-Based Grading Course

These should be posted in the course so students can refer to them at will throughout the class: (1) If applicable, have students carefully read the labor-based contracts for a full understanding; invite questions; (2) Remind students to keep track of their progress to keep abreast of how their grade is calculated; (3) Students need to understand that a labor-based course is not easier because no points are used; they must consistently put in a solid effort to succeed.

Remember: It is the ant's efforts that result in building a beautiful nest, the bodybuilder's efforts that result in lifting record-breaking weights, and the chef's efforts that result in an outstanding meal—without solid effort a superb ending will never result.

Ask Errol!

Errol Craig Sull

Another new year—2022—and we look at past years to see challenges, problems, and difficulties we have overcome in the distance learning environment. This year will also have its share: student demographics, changes in course structures, added or shifted school regulations and guidelines, additional subject information, and introduction of new teaching strategies, as well as being new to teaching online can result in more or new "uh-ohs," "whoas," and "yikes"! As I have for the past 12 years I will offer my input, suggestions, and experience to make 2022 a smooth and enjoyable distance learning teaching experience. (Send your queries to me—erroldistancelearning@gmail.com—for our next issue.)

EXCUSES, EXCUSES, EXCUSES—HOW TO KNOW WHAT'S REAL

Errol, I'm ending this year on a high note as it relates to my online teaching, and part of this success is from a few tips I picked up in your columns—thanks for that! I have solved many student problems, and I've used my total knowledge and experience to allow me nice ownership of my classes. Of course, I wouldn't be writing you if I didn't need your input yet again: how to handle what seems like a growing variety and number of excuses my students give for not turning in an assignment or turning in one late. There used to be the occasional death in the family and once-in-awhile cold, but now I feel like I'm being bombarded with not only these but also COVID, drug overdoses, spending time in jail, baby births, stays in the hospital, and others. Any suggestions on how to tactfully, legally, and efficiently handle this uptick in excuses?

There used to be a joke in online classrooms: faculty could not believe how many grandmothers died, and sometimes three times for one student! Kidding aside, the concern you have is certainly a tricky

Errol Craig Sull,
Faculty, English and Writing Across the Curriculum, Purdue Global University.
Email: erroldistancelearning@gmail.com
(for column submissions)

one. The Family Educational Rights and Privacy Act does not allow certain questions to be asked, each school has its own set of guidelines as how to handle these situations, and the students must not feel you simply don't believe them. Here are some suggestions: (1) Many schools require students to show proof of an illness, death, et cetera; if this is the case you simply need tell a student this is the school's policy, and you must act accordingly; (2) COVID, of course, has become a major problem in all schools, with many students infected. You might be able to obtain a physician's proof of this; also, you can ask questions about the impact on the student's work/have a general conversation (email, text, phone) about the impact it has on the student's life. This can give you a "feel" for the student's veracity; (3) You need determine how many assignments a student has missed/will miss, and make a decision – based on what you can do/what your school policy allows—and ask the student when he or she will get in the missing assignments. As you can see, there is no easy, cut-and-dry answer to this. More often than not, when a school does not have a solid "show proof" requirement it usually comes down to the faculty member giving the student the benefit of the doubt (except, of course, if one student has three grandmothers die!). P.S. Thanks for the nice words about my efforts; that feedback means much!

How Much Writing to Access in Nonwriting Courses

From reading your columns I know you teach English, so no doubt you have a certain bias about the importance of good writing in any course, Errol. That is to be understood. However, I teach two science courses, and my focus, of course, is what my students learn about various science events, genres, projects, and formulae, as well as hydrology, geophysics, and ecology. While I certainly look at a student's overall writing for it making sense, having a logical flow, and proofreading errors that's about it. I started wondering if I'm doing any harm to my students by not spending more time on their writing, yet I also don't want to take away from their science focus. Can you help?

If I could have input on every course taught in every college and university I'd make sure there was one person in a non-composition course whose only responsibility would be to look at a student's writing! But pragmatics must be weighed, and I know folks who teach the sciences, math, economics, computers, et cetera, have to primarily focus on the subject in students' assignments, not their writing, as one would do in an English or composition course. With that said, however, there are a few items you could do that will "up" your cred on helping students with their writing. First, remind students of the important connection between writing on an assignment and writing on the job. It will be judged by others, and the farther up the so-called corporate ladder one goes the more writing one needs to do. Next, you can make a checklist of writing basics that students should keep in mind, such as complete sentences, good spelling, solid grammar, nice proofreading (which you already do); have a few examples of each, both incorrect and correct. You also might want to include this website that discusses the importance of writing in the sciences: https://advice.writing.utoronto.ca/types-of-writing/science/. Finally, let your students help you! Specifically, ask students to assess their writing ability, and perhaps include one paragraph in some of the assignments (the major ones) where students discuss their strengths and weaknesses. You can have various resources available that you can send to individual students or the class that targets the areas needing improvement. These items will help you—while allowing you to remain that science instructor!

RELATING COURSE SUBJECT AND EFFORTS TO THE PROFESSIONAL WORLD

I'm new to distance learning; prior to COVID all my classes were face to face, but I recently learned for the foreseeable future my classes (I teach two introductory math classes at a local university) will all be online. Although it's a new educational environment for me I am getting used to it, and I believe I'm doing a fairly good job. When I taught on the ground campus I always made it a point to remind students of math's importance in their professional careers. I still intend on doing this, but I'm wondering what additional approaches I might take teaching online. Thank you, Errol!

Your dilemma and question are so, so common across all fields! COVID has tossed education on its head, and many instructors have had to adjust to online teaching. Your question is one I relish, for I believe it crucial that students be continually aware of a subject's connection to and importance in their current or future careers. This is what I and other distance learning instructors do, and each is very successful: (1) A benefit of teaching online is the material is available for students 24/7 during a course, so posting reminders—with examples—of how math relates to the job market is a nice plus. (2) With any assignment you might want to have a short note that tells students where this assignment might find value in "the real world of employment." (3) There are several websites that discuss a variety of fields where math majors thrive; this is one: https://www.bestcolleges.com/careers/. (4) Have students tell you—and perhaps the class—how they see your courses helping in their career field. There are often surprises that come in for which instructors had not considered. This also gives students more of a "buy-in "to the classes! (5) Using games and puzzles that incorporate math can be a fun learning experience for students, either part of an assignment or just a bonus in the class. Websites are available with these, such as this: https://mathgames.commons.gc.cuny.edu/. Try one or more of these suggestions; each can make your class not only more exciting but also a great reminder that your courses are appetizers for the entrees of your students' professions.

Remember: To get a plumbing problem fixed—we call a plumber; when our computer has a really bad virus—an information technology expert is brought in; and when our vehicle dies—it's the dealership mechanic who takes over. Knowing when to ask for assistance makes us the stronger and wiser!

And Finally ... *continued from page 68*

resources available to most distance educators. What about DIY—do it yourself?

DIY is the idea of enhancing, creating, or fixing something yourself rather than employing a professional. DIY instructional videos are:

1. *Simple* and cover one idea, such as a single concept
2. *Short*, both in length and in production time – a couple of hours for production of a 3–4-minute video
3. *Unpolished* and *unsophisticated*, and are obviously "homemade"
4. *Personal* because you do it, and it is your creation, not "theirs"

A first question that should be asked is "Are DIY interactive videos effective?" The general answer is YES.

THE TAXONOMY

There is also a taxonomy for DIY interactive instructional videos that relates interaction to the video.

Level 1: The first and most common approach for using a video is to view the video, then interact, usually by discussing it. This approach is the typical way videos are used in a class or online.

Level 2: The second approach is to first interact, then view the video, and next interact again. For example, learners may be asked to explain what they know about a topic such "the lead nurse's role for surgery." Then the video, usually a tutorial, would show the required duties of a lead nurse. Finally, another discussion would be held to reconcile the differences between the first discussion and the second.

Level 3: A third approach is to show the video, then have instructors and learners interact, which would be followed by another clarifying video, or a continuation of the original video. The clarifying video gives more in-depth information about the video's content. Recently, developers have inserted questions during the video for viewers to answer. This modification works great when viewing is by an individual rather than a group.

Level 4: Finally, a fun, simple, and effective approach is called the "What Now…? technique. The *What Now* video technique (also called trigger videos) is a motion media production the presents a dilemma without resolving it. The intent is that the video will lead to an interactive discussion among the group of onsite or online learners for which it was intended. The dilemma can be of many kinds—ethical, professional, moral, financial, technical, social or organizational.

For any type of DIY video—entertainment, informative, or persuasive—only a few ingredients are necessary. First, one needs an **idea**. What is the problem, the situation, or the event to be the basis for the DIY video? Next, the idea should be made real by writing a *script*—a script is a video production plan with a written explanation of the motion segments and the narrative.

Next a simple *computer* with basic video production software is needed—certainly free software. Next, a video *camera* is needed. Today, the best choice for a DIY video is the cell phone. Finally, a little *time*. The rule of thumb is that a DIY video should be about 3–4 minutes long and take 3-4 hours or less to produce.

Sound simple, well of course it is not. To start, grab your iPhone, shoot some footage, transfer it to a computer, do simple editing, and take a look. Of course, there are tutorials available online, but today, trial and error is fun and does not cost anything.

And finally, to paraphrase Coleridge, "it is not the video which we have viewed, but that to which we remember."

And Finally ...

Interactive Instructional Videos

Michael Simonson

For some reason, interactive videos are now a big thing. Could it be that videographers are starting to read the research? Or is this a new spin on the old idea.

First, instructional videos are "recorded content with motion that provides detailed information on how to meet a specific educational challenge, such as *knowing* something, being able to *do* something, or *feeling* something—the three domains of learning—cognitive, psychomotor, affective.

Generally, traditional instructional videos (films actually) tended to be about 27–28 minutes long, presented about a multifaceted topic, and were usually viewed in a classroom situation—because there was no way to see the video or film at home.

The content of a traditional instructional films, if well done, could be divided into about five subideas. These ideas, when viewed in sequence, provided a fairly comprehensive presentation of the topic.

Instructional videos and films were almost always produced by professional film crews or videographers working from a detailed script with a talented acting crew. Do you remember "An Occurrence at Owl Creek Bridge?" If you haven't seen it, look it up on YouTube and watch.

Interaction, the new spin on instructional videos, certainly sounds good. Interaction is communication or direct involvement with someone or something—it is the way people affect one another. For example, the two ended their interaction with a hug.

Interactive instructional video is instruction using video that enables people to understand, do, or feel something, such as solving a problem, building a fence, or expressing empathy, with interaction added. And as with all interaction, there is something for viewers to do—they interact.

Often, professional, or semi-professional instructional videos are produced by a team. Having professional help is great, but expensive help is often beyond the

Michael Simonson, Editor, *Distance Learning*, Professor, Instructional Technology and Distance Education, Fischler College of Education, Nova Southeastern University, 3301 College Avenue, Fort Lauderdale, FL 33314. Telephone: (954) 262-8563. E-mail: simsmich@nova.edu

... continues on page 67